Five-to-Be-Alive: The Values Plan for Living Your Best Life

A Values Gals Guide

By Amy Bailey and Liz Stubbs

Five-to-Be-Alive:
The Values Plan for Living Your Best Life

A Values Gals Guide

Copyright © 2010. Values Innovations, Inc.

All rights reserved. Published by Values Innovations, Inc.
www.thevaluesgals.com

Five-to-Be-Alive™ and The Values Gals™ are trademarks of Values Innovations, Inc.

Book cover design by Rebecca Morgan: www.girlwerk.com.

All photos in the book are courtesy
Amy Bailey and Liz Stubbs and may not be duplicated without written permission.

ISBN: 978-0-615-33986-3

Acclaim for *Five-to-Be-Alive: The Values Plan for Living Your Best Life*

"For the short-tempered, underpaid, bogged down and overweight, the stepping stones to a better life begin with five core values in this book, *Five-to-Be-Alive: The Values Plan for Living Your Best Life*. Let Amy and Liz guide you through the basics and introduce the person you see in the mirror to the happier, healthier, wealthier and wiser soul you always expected to be."
–Karen Denny, wife, mom and Lifestyle and Food Editor for the McClatchy-Tribune News Service.

"Nothing plays a greater role than our values in shaping who we are and how we live our lives. In Five-to-Be-Alive, the Values Gals offer us invaluable tips on how to face any challenge on the road to becoming our best selves."
—Spencer Christian, host on ABC-TV's The View From the Bay (San Francisco)

"Our busy lives can feel like a whirlwind of elusive dreams and a vortex of constant responsibilities with a healthy smattering of the unexpected. It's easy to feel like our passions and dreams take a backseat to the hectic realities of day-to-day. But we can all live our best lives and have dreams with deadlines, when we bring values into our action plan. The Values Gals walk us through easy steps to craft personalized values plans to excel at any goal and in any situation."
—Dr. Marty Becker, Resident veterinarian on Good Morning America and The Dr. Oz Show, nationally

syndicated columnist, and author of 20 pet books including four New York Times bestsellers.

"Daily to-do's seem overwhelming? Fretting over those couple of extra pounds? Do you despair that your childhood dreams will never materialize into reality? The Five-to-Be-Alive Values Plan gets to the core of where we get stuck and helps you find unexpected ways to move forward. The Five-to-Be-Alive get us on track to achieve and maintain any goal we set. Liz Stubbs and Amy Bailey create an action plan specifically designed for you."
—*Cooper Lawrence, Author and Television & Radio Personality*

In Gratitude

I am deeply grateful to the many people who have provided support during the writing of our book or who influenced what my fingers typed as I wrote. I am most grateful to my family—my husband Brian and our two children Chase and Claire—for your patience, love, support and understanding. Thanks to our dog Chip who boosted my spirits with happy smiles, tail wags and tummy rub opportunities during much needed breaks. I owe much to my parents—a solid, strong values foundation and the confidence to be "me" is the greatest gift you have ever given me—I can't thank you enough for that. To my extended family and others who influenced me over the years—I thank you for the examples you set that helped me understand what really matters. To Irving Stubbs, who was responsible for getting me involved in the business of values—I thank you for inspiring me to care about making a difference through this work. To friends who care about me and therefore what I do—your unconditional and thoughtful support has, at times, humbled me—I thank you simply for being there. And lastly, to Liz, my co-author, for being a great partner to work with; for understanding and tolerating my Type-A tendencies; for your patience with my scattered calendar and delays that it caused; and for your creativity, adaptability and open mind.–AMY

No dream or endeavor lives without the support of generous spirits. I want to first thank my boyfriend, Mark, who, on one of our first dates years ago, asked me what my values were… and I didn't have a ready answer! Thus starting my adult values journey. A lifetime of thanks goes to my parents who consciously lived in accord with their values and led by example. To Jane Cole, a world of thanks for being such a creative and enthusiastic consultant, contributor and supporter since before we became the Values Gals. I am daily grateful to my dog Zoe, who is a wise and wonderful teacher and who inspires me to be a better person and to live as steadfastly in line with my values as she does. To Spencer Christian for being such a fabulous values champion and for helping us bring our message to a wider audience. Thank you, Amy, for having such a positive energy, being an endless source of ideas and solutions, and having a priceless sense of humor no matter how large our to-do list grows! And thank you to all my family and friends who have generously shared their time, their connections, and their good energy to help us engage in the values conversation.—Liz

IN GRATITUDE 5

A FEW WORDS BEFORE WE BEGIN… 13

CHAPTER 1 21

VALUES: THE BASICS—WHAT ARE VALUES AND WHERE DO THEY COME FROM? 21

WHAT ARE VALUES? 21
WHERE DO OUR VALUES COME FROM? 24
VALUES TUNE-UP 32

CHAPTER 2 43

BENEFITS TO LIVING A VALUES-DRIVEN LIFE 43

I. ME, MYSELF AND I 46
II. FAMILY 50
III. AT THE OFFICE 58
IV. COMMUNITY 65
V. FRIENDS 70
VI. THE VALUE OF VALUES 75

CHAPTER 3 78

THE CORE FIVE—OUR FIVE-TO-BE-ALIVE VALUES 78

OUR BEST-LIFE DESIGN? A COOKIE 80
WHAT ARE THE FIVE-TO-BE-ALIVE VALUES? 81
ACCOUNTABILITY 82
THE BASICS 82
ALIGNMENT 84

WHY ACCOUNTABILITY? 88
SELF-RESPECT 91
THE BASICS 91
ALIGNMENT 91
WHY SELF-RESPECT? 93
LOVE 96
THE BASICS 96
ALIGNMENT 97
WHY LOVE? 98
HAPPINESS 99
THE BASICS 99
ALIGNMENT 103
WHY HAPPINESS? 106
GRATITUDE 106
THE BASICS 106
ALIGNMENT 107
WHY GRATITUDE? 109
FIVE-TO-BE-ALIVE IN THE REAL WORLD 110
OUTSIDE INFLUENCES 111
FAMILY 111
SCHOOL 112
COMMUNITY 112
RELIGION 113
WORK 113

CHAPTER 4 115

SEEING OUR VALUES 115

SEEING OUR VALUES: PERSONAL VALUES ASSESSMENT 119
VALUES AS DAILY TOOLS: SEEING BENEFITS 121
<u>I want to feed myself and my family healthily, but we are on a tight budget.</u>..129
<u>I want to exercise regularly but don't have the time.</u> 130
<u>My family doesn't spend any time together—we're all too busy.</u>.....130
<u>My love life has gone stale.</u>..131
<u>I'd like to lose a couple pounds.</u> 132

I wish I felt younger. 133
I'm exhausted all the time—I want to feel less tired. 133
I want to find work that I enjoy and pays the bills. 134

CHAPTER 5 136

PERSONAL VALUES PLANS—BLUEPRINT FOR ALIGNING WITH OUR FIVE-TO-BE-ALIVE VALUES 136

PERSONAL VALUES PLAN: OVERVIEW 138
PERSONAL VALUES PLAN: SAMPLE 138
PERSONAL VALUES PLAN: TEMPLATE FOR PERSONAL GOALS 146

CHAPTER 6 151

THE FIVE IN PRACTICE: REACHING YOUR GOALS 151

YOUR FIVE-TO-BE-ALIVE FOR BETTER HEALTH 152
OTHER VALUES THAT WILL HELP YOU REACH YOUR BETTER HEALTH GOAL 156
A FEW PRACTICAL STEPS TOWARDS BETTER HEALTH 157
HELPFUL RESOURCES 157
PERSONAL STORY: OPTIMIZING AND MAINTAINING MY BEST HEALTH ... 158
YOUR FIVE-TO-BE-ALIVE FOR GREEN LIVING 162
OTHER VALUES THAT WILL HELP YOU REACH YOUR GREEN LIVING GOAL 166
A FEW PRACTICAL STEPS TOWARDS GREEN LIVING 167
HELPFUL RESOURCES 167
PERSONAL STORY: GETTING TO A GREENER EXISTENCE 167
YOUR FIVE-TO-BE-ALIVE FOR IMPROVED FINANCIAL STATION 172
OTHER VALUES THAT WILL HELP YOU REACH YOUR IMPROVED FINANCIAL STATION GOAL 175
A FEW PRACTICAL STEPS TOWARDS IMPROVING YOUR FINANCIAL STATION 176
HELPFUL RESOURCES 176
PERSONAL STORY: EARNING HARD-WON FINANCIAL FREEDOM 177
YOUR FIVE-TO-BE-ALIVE FOR REALIZING OUR DREAMS 182

OTHER VALUES THAT WILL HELP YOU REACH YOUR GOAL OF REALIZING YOUR DREAMS 185
A FEW PRACTICAL STEPS TOWARDS REALIZING OUR DREAMS 186
HELPFUL RESOURCES 186
PERSONAL STORY: LISTENING TO MY COURAGE TO FOLLOW MY CAREER DREAMS 187
PERSONAL STORY: MID-LIFE PROFESSIONAL SHIFT—CREATING A CAREER FROM A CHILDHOOD DREAM: 190
YOUR FIVE-TO-BE-ALIVE FOR BETTER RELATIONSHIPS 194
OTHER VALUES THAT WILL HELP YOU HAVE BETTER RELATIONSHIPS .. 198
A FEW PRACTICAL STEPS FOR ACHIEVING BETTER RELATIONSHIPS 200
HELPFUL TIPS/RESOURCES 201
PERSONAL STORY: MAKING TRAVEL WITH FAMILY A PRIORITY 202
YOUR FIVE-TO-BE-ALIVE FOR CAREER/WORK IMPROVEMENTS 208
OTHER VALUES FOR ACHIEVING WORK OR CAREER PATH IMPROVEMENTS 212
A FEW PRACTICAL STEPS FOR MAKING CAREER/WORK IMPROVEMENTS 214
HELPFUL TIPS/RESOURCES 215
PERSONAL STORY: FOCUSING ON FULFILLING WORK 216
YOUR FIVE-TO-BE-ALIVE FOR FINDING/PRESERVING LOVE 221
OTHER VALUES FOR FINDING/PRESERVING LOVE 224
A FEW PRACTICAL STEPS FOR FINDING/PRESERVING LOVE 226
HELPFUL TIPS/RESOURCES 227
PERSONAL STORY: THE JOURNEY OF LOVING OUR WAY THROUGH CHALLENGES 228
YOUR FIVE-TO-BE-ALIVE FOR SIMPLIFYING YOUR LIFE 233
OTHER VALUES THAT WILL HELP YOU SIMPLIFY YOUR LIFE 237
A FEW PRACTICAL STEPS FOR SIMPLIFYING YOUR LIFE 238
HELPFUL TIPS/RESOURCES 240
PERSONAL STORY: ORGANIZING AND STREAMLINING MY HOME LIFE TO REDUCE STRESS 241
YOUR FIVE-TO-BE-ALIVE FOR WEIGHT LOSS 248
OTHER VALUES THAT WILL HELP YOU REACH YOUR WEIGHT LOSS GOAL 252
A FEW PRACTICAL STEPS FOR LOSING WEIGHT* 253
HELPFUL RESOURCES 255
PERSONAL STORY: LOSING THAT BABY WEIGHT 257
PERSONAL STORY: COMING TO TERMS WITH BEING "JUST MOM" 261

Personal Story: My Mentor, the Marathon 265
Personal Story: The Values of a New Start 268
Personal Story: Overcoming the Adversity of a Significant Health Issue 273

CHAPTER 7—LET'S RECAP..**283**

A FEW WORDS BEFORE WE BEGIN...

Values are the most essential tool in helping us create our best possible lives. And this book is the most essential tool for helping understand that. There are no tricks, no special formulas, no complicated processes to surrender to, no expensive gadget to buy or service to subscribe to.

Values are not a common topic of conversation. Often we go about our lives fairly unconscious of our values. Not until something unexpected happens do we get that instant perspective check on our lives. We get up each morning, we go to work, we take care of our families, support our friends, play with our pets; we do our errands and chores, we pay our bills, and somewhere in the mix we may, if we're lucky, find a little time to recreate and relax. But then, out of the blue, a family member dies in a car accident, we lose our job, the bank threatens to foreclose on our house, our child is diagnosed with a serious illness, a neighbor is robbed at gunpoint, a tornado destroys our home.

When the unpleasant surprises come, we are reminded how quickly life can change. How our dreams can suddenly be shattered. How the picture we thought we had for the future might be radically different from now on. What we don't recognize as readily is how, quite often, these upsetting events are also occasions for us to count our blessings. When we realize how fortunate we are to enjoy the aspects of our life that truly make us happy and rich—good health, love, friends, family, laughter—we become newly conscious of how much we really have to be grateful for.

So where do values play in to these scenarios? Values are invaluable assets that help us constructively manage upsets and stay balanced when these shocking and life-altering events happen to us and to our loved ones. They are not just powerful in extreme situations, however. Values are critical resources for helping us as we move through the day-to-dayness of our lives. Our values keep us on track with the kind of person we want to be and on the path to living the kind of life we dream of living.

A brief aside here: when we speak about values, we are not talking about the kind of judgment-laden terms like "family values" that have been popularized in recent political campaigns. When we discuss values, we are talking about the core principles that guide our choices and behaviors. We explore the term in more detail in Chapter One.

Every person in this world has adopted and developed, perhaps somewhat subconsciously, a set of values that are as individual and unique as we each are. We'll use ourselves as examples. We are Amy and Liz, the Values Gals. Amy is married and a mother to two children, a son and a daughter. Liz is in a relationship with her boyfriend and is parent to a 65-pound four-legged furry pup. Amy's professional background is in the business/corporate world. Liz's professional background is in the freelance video/film and writing world. We both are into traveling, health, fitness and family. And we also differ in certain respects, approaches and backgrounds. Involved in the values world for several years now, we have learned through our experiences, research and work what a life-changing impact our practice of values can have. We co-wrote this book to share our life-changing experiences with the practice of values—five key values in particular. You may distinguish our different styles of writing as you read though this book. We've not attempted nor wanted to change one another's voice. We think that's a great example of how, just as with values sets, we can each bring something different to the party AND still be united on the core theme and objective of our book.

My (Liz's) set of values is not identical to Amy's values. Further, my value set is not exactly the same as my boyfriend's. Amy's husband may have different values priorities. And that's the way it should be. We each have a customized personal values system. But most of us do share a set of core values. Most people, we have found, agree that love and integrity are key values that we all believe guide our life decisions and our behaviors. And while we may rank the importance of individual values differently–my top ten may look a little different than Amy's–most people agree on the notion that positive values practice is a good thing.

But surprise, surprise! What we typically list as our values on paper is not always what we practice when living our day-to-day routines. Yes, we think certain values are important to practice, but when the rubber hits the road, we don't always act in alignment with those values. For example, honesty and integrity are critically important values for me to practice and live by. Even though honesty may not always seem easy, I've seen too much upset come from dishonesty. That said, am I always honest in practice? I may be tempted to exaggerate or underestimate from time to time—how many cookies I ate, how much I weigh, how much I paid for a pair of shoes, do I like so and so's new haircut—my answers to those questions may shift from the truth a tad depending on who's asking. However, in the big picture, I usually am and have proven to be a person of integrity who tells the truth, even when it's uncomfortable. It would be easy to only admit to one cookie, select a weight I want to be versus what I am, offer up a less expensive number when asked about my shoes if I felt I had been indulgent or respond "yes" without thinking to an inquiry about whether I like something or not. *(For the record, I ate two cookies, I don't own scales so I don't know how much I weigh but I know my clothes still fit from years ago, I paid $75 for my last pair of shoes, and, the haircut was surprising but I did like it.).*

It's convenient to assume that no harm would be done to utter half-truths or to brush off not living up to what we think or want our values standards to be–especially when the issue seems to be of no or little consequence. But we've both been there, either personally involved or as a witness, and it's a slippery slope. You'll read more about that slippery slope in the book.

Perhaps the most effective way we can use values is to consciously harness their power to help us live our best possible life. Reawakening to our values can make our lives generally and infinitely better. But there are five core values in particular, that when mindfully practiced, can help each of us to live the life of our dreams—we call them our Five-to-Be-Alive values. Living in alignment with the Five-to-Be-Alive, no matter what surprises come our way, we can all live our best possible lives.

In this book, we offer you the opportunity to:

- Discover your personal values system.
- Assess how much or how little you practice the values that are important to you.
- Build mindfulness and practice of the values you espouse.
- Develop personalized strategies for using the Five-to-Be-Alive to accomplish any goal.
- Create a life-long practice of the Five-to-Be-Alive to live your best possible life.

In order to reap the benefits of the Five-to-Be-Alive values system, you have to **PRACTICE** them. This message is reinforced in the book over and over again. Intentionally. It's one thing to agree with what we discuss in the book but to change your life in any way—a little or a lot—you must put the Five-to-Be-Alive in action. Everyday. Even if the tweaks you make are minor, they can add up to big benefits.

The benefits are both immediate and long-term when you adopt our approach of investigating and affirming the role our values play in truly reaching our life's goals. Everyone, yes, **EVERYONE** can benefit from the Five-to-Be-Alive!

- If you are feeling stuck and unable to move forward in work, in relationships, in goals, or toward your dreams, regular attention to and practice of the Five-to-Be-Alive can bring powerful positive change to whatever your situation might be. We show you how.
- If you have lost your hope or drive to living the life you once dreamed of—a life of health and happiness and love—the Five-to-Be-Alive can renew your energy to start living fully. We show you how.

- If your life is already pretty incredible and you feel very lucky and happy with how you are already living, the Five-to-Be-Alive can take you to a heightened experience of living fully and living well all while opening new opportunities along the way. We show you how.

Ready to live your best possible life? Read on!

Five-to-Be-Alive: The Values Plan for Living Your Best Life

A Values Gals Guide

Chapter 1

Values: The Basics—What Are Values and Where Do They Come From?

What Are Values?

The very first thing we need to do to get started is to be clear how we are using the term "values." Presently, the word tends to conjure up all things financial rather than what this book is about—the values we can actually control—that is to say *our values*. We are not, however, talking about stock market portfolios, how much our homes are worth, the interest we are earning on all our accounts—these monetary things over which we have very little control. We are talking about our *personal values*, those qualities that make us who we are and what our character is built upon—the values over which we have **complete** control.

Simply stated, values are the standards by which we choose to live our lives. People use terms like morals, principles, beliefs and personal philosophy as synonyms for the term values. The word preference doesn't really matter (although we like "values"). What does matter is that you know what your values are and that you practice them in a way that allows you to get the most out of your life.

Let's take a second to let that thought sink in. Our values—what they are and how we practice them—are the key to getting the most out of our life, to living the fullest life we can imagine.

Our values are what help us to determine what is right or wrong, good or bad and what actions we should or shouldn't take. These guiding principles of ours can be positive and constructive: honesty, integrity, happiness, kindness, gratitude, accountability, fairness, love, self-respect. Or they can be negative and destructive: greed, rudeness, indifference, dishonesty, negligence, meanness, impatience, selfishness, apathy.

Values are at the core of who we are as people. They drive the way in which we behave and the decisions we make every day. We make snap decisions all the time—decisions we seem to scarcely think about—but the values that have been instilled in us over time by mentors, influential individuals in our lives, and other media that we are exposed to guide our reactions and behaviors.

The degree to which we practice our values in any given moment can vary. In addition, how we want to act and how we do act are often at odds with one another. We sometimes use different values under stress, for example. Anyone who has ever been cut off in traffic, having to slam on the brakes to prevent a collision, might know what we're talking about. Even if we normally wouldn't swear in anger or drive aggressively, we might in response to a rude driver. In a bad economy we see people under financial strain make desperate choices, perhaps acting in dishonest or illegal ways in order to make a buck to pay the rent. The normally patient, kind parents—when sleep-deprived and juggling too many responsibilities—will snap at their children or friends in an uncaring or rude manner. In the best of times we often practice our best values, and in the worst of times, we might practice just the opposite.

Take a minute to think about how you might feel and what your interactions with others might look like if you experienced any of the following:

- You are laid off from your job.
- You have been up several nights in a row tending to a sick child.
- You suffer an injury that causes pain and long-term physical limitations.
- You discover your child has been lying to you and/or breaking your rules.
- You fall behind on an important payment.
- A close relative falls ill and the prognosis is bleak for survival.
- Your spouse leaves you.
- You are hit with an unexpected, very costly home or car repair.
- Your friends are excluding you from social activities.

In any of these scenarios, it would be normal to feel sadness, disappointment, fear, grief, frustration and stress. No one would expect happiness from someone who just lost a job or discovered a loved one was terminally ill. When faced with challenges such as the above, it is often quite difficult to "be ourselves."

Negative situations often negatively impact the manner in which we interact with others. The way we normally behave or strive to behave falls by the wayside when something is not right in our lives. We may be driven to behave dishonestly, telling our landlord that we mailed our rent check when we did not in order to buy some time. When relationships hit rocky patches we often say things we later wish we hadn't. Out of hurt, anger or humiliation, we lash out with unkind, vengeful words. During times of sadness or grief we sometimes close ourselves off from others and let ourselves feel like victims. We blame others rather than seek out constructive steps we can take to help ourselves or to help those who are suffering. It is as important to understand what affects the practice of our values as it is to understand what our values are.

Where Do Our Values Come From?
Our values are not static. They can change. These changes can be temporary and deviate from the norm due to our mood, our environment, and other situational factors. They can also go through more permanent changes. Our values can and do evolve over time. With age comes wisdom, or so they say, and the more we learn about life the more we come to know ourselves. Children who are introverts often become extroverts as adults. And extroverted children may prefer to fly a little more under the radar as adults. Over time, we discover and are exposed to so many things that play into the values we choose as our "core values"—the values that are the most important to us. As we learn what traits we like or don't like in people, what issues we think are important versus just blips on the screen, and what we want to be when we "grow up" our values get shaped in the process. Many other influences along the way shape our values into being: religion, politics, environment, family, peer groups and media exposure are all powerful influencers.

It is true that many of our values are taught to us at a young age and may feel resistant to change, having been with us our whole lives. It is common for parents to begin teaching values right away by modeling the behaviors we want our children to possess:

- We sing and talk to infants who understand nothing we say, knowing they will eventually; in the meantime, we hope that whatever we're saying or doing is sinking in.
- We say "thank you" to babies when they hand us a toy, hoping to instill good manners and an almost innate desire to express gratitude.
- We encourage smiles maybe because they are cute, but aren't we also encouraging happiness?
- We say "yes" and "no" with equal enthusiasm so that our children understand what is acceptable or not, dangerous or safe, good or bad.

Many children show values like compassion, kindness, gratitude and honesty, sometimes brutal honesty, from a very young age, making experts wonder if some values are intrinsic. Studies have shown that babies, in their responses to various stimuli, show compassion and empathy well before they can understand what these words mean. Some hold the belief that we are "born good." If this is the case, it is safe to reason that from there we can keep on that path of developing a positive set of values or go in the other direction if we don't have positive role models, experiences and exposures to help reinforce that intrinsic good.

In a discussion about values it is important to acknowledge what influences our values. Our religious affiliation, political leanings, income level, race, gender, the type of education we've received or degree we hold, our job title or our marital status are *not* absolute indicators of what types of values we practice. People who, on the outside, appear to have many similarities often behave very differently. Why? Because of their values. And what causes them to behave very differently often are the influences they have experienced in their lives.

For example, many CEOs have watched their companies fall because of their greed and dishonest business practices. In contrast, other CEOs have seen their businesses thrive and achieve success beyond anyone's expectations due to their strong leadership guided by honesty and accountability. With different values come different results. We have seen legislators turn things around for their states, lowering unemployment and cleaning up dangerous neighborhoods. We've also seen legislators shamefully stepping down after being caught in fraudulent, illegal matters. Similar positions, different values, different outcomes. The same can be said about religious leaders, teachers, esteemed community members and "good parents" —for every positive story there is one that is the polar opposite. The role we play in business or in the community is not the driving force for our doing good or bad. Values drive behaviors and our values-driven behaviors reveal who we really are.

But where do our values come from? What are the influences? While our religious affiliation, political leanings, income level, race, gender, the type of education we've received or degree we hold, our job title or our marital status may _influence our values practice_ they alone _do not define_ what our personal values are.

When we make friendships, build relationships or decide to join some sort of group, we tend to gravitate towards people with whom we have common interests or beliefs. We align ourselves with a given religion and select places of worship this way. We support political parties or candidates and vote this way. Our strongest friendships and relationships often tend to be with people who hold similar beliefs and interests as we do. These connections bring us together, and it is in these groups or with these people that our values get influenced and shaped and reinforced.

- *Family influences our values.* Parents might be the biggest influencers on a child's values system. In several surveys, the majority of children responded that when they are faced with a challenge and aren't sure what to do, the question they ask themselves most often is "what would my parents want me to do?"

- *Religion influences our values.* Those who seek regular religious guidance are shaped by what they are taught and will turn to those teachings to guide them when they don't know what to do. They might ask themselves "what does the Bible say about this?" Many religious teachings do reinforce the practice of positive values. However, extreme positions or religions sometimes promote intolerance or even hateful postures towards other religious groups or cultures. Intolerance and hate are also values, just destructive ones—ones that never lead to a greater good.

- *Politics influences our values.* We often select our political party based on our strong feelings about certain issues like taxes, capital punishment, abortion, education and healthcare. Once we've aligned ourselves with a given party and have voted for certain leaders, we look to that party and those leaders as examples to follow. They are like us, we tell ourselves, because we believe the same things about the issues that are important to us. Therefore, we may find ourselves emulating those leaders. Now if they are acting honestly, accountably and fairly, there is no cause for concern. But when these leaders do not act with integrity, what happens or what could potentially happen?

- **Educators influence our values.** Teachers are with children often as much as or longer than their own parents on the days they attend school. They have a tremendous influence on children's values—by what they teach, what they positively or negatively reinforce, what they are willing to tolerate as acceptable behaviors and what values they model themselves every day in the classroom. Most adults remember the teachers they loved and the teachers they hated as kids. Many of the hated ones were viewed as unkind, unfair, mean and disrespectful to them.

- **Communities influence our values.** Where we live, work, and play has an impact on our values. When we see neighbors helping other neighbors it reinforces kindness. When children play together, taking turns, sharing toys and exhibiting fairness it reinforces what it takes to get along in relationships. When we keep our homes and properties in good repair we reinforce responsibility and respect for what we own. Interacting with community members in civil ways—in line at the grocery store, on the sidewalk, doing business with our banks—we encourage that behavior. And that has a domino effect.

A sense of community is a big plus in neighborhoods.

As we set examples for those around us to follow, we establish a norm of civility in our community and in our workplace by being kind, respectful and responsible towards those we know well and those we happen to meet in passing.

- **Friends and colleagues influence our values.** People with whom we choose to interact—our friends—affect our values as do the people with whom we work. Peer pressure is not limited to our youth, but it tends to prevail more at that point in our lives than in adulthood. Or does it? People want to "belong." Most do not want to cause controversy or spark confrontations by being the odd man out. Children are told to "just say no" when it comes to participating in various nefarious activities. This mantra should be used far more often by kids *and* adults.

  - When a group is being unkind to

others, rude, disrespectful, intolerant or otherwise exhibiting less than stellar behavior by going along with the crowd, you are essentially supporting it by being a part of the group even if you don't actively participate.
- Letting a boss treat you or others in a disrespectful manner reinforces that it's okay to do so.
- If you treat your employees or coworkers with respect, you will get more out of them, and you will relate to them better.

Doing nothing does, in fact, result in something and that something is the reinforcement that these negative values practices are acceptable.
As friends and colleagues, we can be great examples of positive values practice.

- When, as the boss, you show up to work on time or as an employee you meet your deadline, you set that responsible example.
- When, as a friend, you advise another friend against making a poor choice or abstain from that poor choice yourself you are reinforcing courage and personal accountability. If you don't keep your commitments with your friends, you can expect the same from them.
- When you set a good example for your employees or peers you should not be surprised when you see the same behaviors from them.

People are always watching how others behave—we are often much better at emulating behaviors than we are at heeding words of advice when the two are not in agreement.

- **The media influences our values.** Television, the Internet, newspapers, magazines, music and movies have a tremendous impact on their audience, especially children. We are bombarded with images and stories of people behaving badly:
    - Mothers murder their children then go out drinking with friends later that night;
    - Athletes take steroids then lie about it or behave badly off the field or court and lament the pressure to always be a role model;
    - Celebrities regularly check themselves into rehab;
    - Reality television often captures the ugly sides of people;
    - News shows that lean to the left or right lambaste those that don't lean in their direction;
    - Movies, television and music entertainment is filled with, and often seems to glorify, violence, profanity, sex and greed. Furthermore, the media typically does not present a view that denunciates these behaviors, for the media is supposed to be unbiased and/or it is assumed the audience will know what is right or wrong, good or bad or what is simply for entertainment purposes, and not an advocacy of anything being aired.

In painting the picture of how values impact our lives, it is important to not only be consciously *aware of what our values are* but *who and what influences them*—both in a positive way and a negative one. Being consciously aware is something that takes a little practice. We are constantly being guided by our values as we move about our lives and hopefully, the majority of the time, this results in us being generally happy with the way our lives are going and the state of our relationships. It's very easy, however, to take our values system for granted. We go about our busy lives not really thinking about our values, or if we do think about them, we tend to believe that they are fine, especially if everything seems to be generally okay.

Values Tune-Up

Much like the cars we drive, our values system may need a tune-up every now and then. As part of that tune-up, of our becoming attentive to the state of our values practice, we may determine that everything, indeed, is in good working order, and we can keep purring along doing what we've been doing. Other times, and often times however, we will find that a little tweaking is necessary. If you've snapped at your spouse or your child, maybe an apology is in order. If you forgot to say thank you or were impatient with a sales clerk, a little self-awareness might help you remember to be mindful the next time you're out shopping. The tweaks may be minor—little improvements that you can make—or you may find that some bigger changes are required. But in order to really key in on the changes that might be beneficial to us, we must understand the answer to the question "what are values?"

Later in this book we focus very specifically on five particular values that we believe play a key role in being successful with any goal you are trying to reach, but we'd be remiss if we failed to mention the myriad other values that we embody and acknowledge the role they play in our everyday lives. Earlier, we mentioned that values are the standards by which we live our lives. Whether we are consciously aware of them or not, they are the drivers for our actions and behaviors, and it would behoove us to know which ones are the most important to us. Understanding what they *are* and what they *mean* is imperative.

For your consideration, we have included a bulleted list of values, along with some simple definitions. It is crucial to underscore again that *values belong to individuals.* You hold the rights to your values. No one can dictate to you which ones are the most important or what values you should choose as your own. We encourage you, then, to take the time to define for yourself what these values mean to you.

Our definitions are meant to serve as a catalyst for your personal thought, allowing you to expand upon what you read here to personalize how important each value is in your life. You may find that you are in agreement with our definitions, which is fine, but we encourage you to think beyond just what we've written; to ponder whether any of these values need more clarification or definition to accurately convey what they mean to *you.* We have provided some questions and statements along with each value to help you understand, think about and visualize when you might feel or practice these values. Later in the book we will also explore some of these values in further detail.

- *Happiness*—a state of mind or feeling of contentment, pleasure, satisfaction, fulfillment or joy.

    - *What would your perfect day look like?*
    - *What emotions do you feel when you are spending time with friends, family or people you care about?*
    - *It brings me joy to take good care of my family.*

- *Self-Respect*—a regard for our own self; an apt confidence and admiration in our own character.

    - *What do people have on the inside that makes them want to exercise and care about their well-being?*
    - *After being treated unkindly by her boyfriend on several dates she told him she no longer wanted to see him.*

- *Gratitude*—the feeling of being thankful or appreciative.

    - *I have a nice home, kind friends, a loving family and many opportunities to be successful in my life.*
    - *When her husband was ill in the hospital neighbors organized a schedule to provide meals for her family.*

- *Accountability*—the state of being responsible, answerable or liable.

    - *The workers showed up every day on time, worked hard and stayed on task.*

- When you realize you've made a mistake that may impact others, do you communicate it and accept whatever consequences there may be, or do you try to cover it up, blame someone else or make excuses?
- *Love*—a feeling of deep, tender affection for someone; a strong fondness, enthusiasm or interest for anything.
  - People we may love: parents, children, our pets & friends.
  - Hobbies/interests/things we may love: traveling, antiquing, knitting, coffee, chocolate, running, hiking & reading.
  - Think of someone or something that you can't imagine not being in your world or your life. You probably feel some kind of love for this activity, person or thing.
- *Honesty*—a state of being truthful, sincere or free of deceit.
  - Do you ever cheat? Tell lies? Exaggerate the truth? Misrepresent what you see or do? These are all examples of dishonest practices.
  - Honesty is communicating what you see, hear, feel or do in a way that accurately represents the facts.
- *Integrity*—adherence to a set of positive values; the sum of the constructive values that we practice.

- *People of integrity are often people we trust, believe to be honest, fair, responsible and considerate people.*
- *When you have integrity you strive to do what is right, not just for yourself but also for a greater good.*

- **Fairness**—to be just or unbiased; to play by the rules.

  - *It is fair for siblings to take turns using toys, a family computer or getting to choose what movie to watch.*
  - *Fairness is upholding what's right—it's sticking to the rules of the game.*

- **Kindness**—to be nice, helpful or good to someone;

  - *Have you ever held the door for someone? Let someone go ahead of you in line? Listened to a child's long-winded, meandering story about their day?*
  - *Kindness is shown by the resident who shovels an elderly neighbor's driveway after a big snow storm.*

- **Civility**—polite actions or expressions; showing courtesy or good manners;

  - *Allowing someone to merge into traffic in front of you; not interrupting when someone is speaking; saying 'please' and 'thank you' are all ways we express civility.*

- How do you feel when someone bumps into you in passing and doesn't say "Excuse me" or "I'm sorry"? How about when someone passes through a door and lets it slam back in your face rather than hold it open for you?

- **Achievement**—the act of attaining, accomplishing or finishing something; to perform in a way that gets results.

    - How do you know when you've achieved something? Is your to-do list completely checked off? Do you get a report card or evaluation that conveys it? Are you promoted? Do your kids tell you in some way?
    - Achieving may mean that we are doing well, succeeding, reaching a goal, completing a task or realizing some state of being, such as being happy. What does it mean to achieve in your life?

- **Freedom**—the power to make choices and decisions without, or with minimal, constraint, outside control, interference or unjust regulation.

    - The Constitution of the United States outlines freedoms such as freedom of speech, freedom of religion and the freedom of the press. These are rights that we have as citizens.
    - Being able to make choices in our lives means we have freedoms. What choices

do you make or have that you consider to be freedoms?

- ***Empathy**—identifying with the feelings, experiences, thoughts or mind-sets of others.*

    - *How does it make you feel when someone you care about is sad, grieving or brokenhearted? Are you able to relate to their suffering and show an understanding through your actions or your words?*
    - *Empathy can be expressed without words. You can convey your understanding with a smile, a hug or a knowing glance or nod.*

- ***Generosity**—the willingness and desire to give in abundance.*

    - *We often feel people are generous when we receive gifts on our birthdays or for holidays. Gift-giving is one way to be generous.*
    - *People can be generous with their time, their talent, their knowledge, their sacrifice or their love. One need not give material objects or money to be generous.*

After giving some thought to this exercise, we hope you now have a better understanding of what values are, what it means to practice them and, more importantly, what values mean to you. You may also have a clearer picture as to how you practice your values in your everyday life and when you are faced with a challenge.

We won't explore all the values we defined here—in fact, we will focus heavily on just five specific values. These five key values will help you reach any goal you set for your life. Usually, when we set goals or make decisions, especially complex ones, many values come into play. Having a broader understanding of what your values are and how they affect the little and big choices in your life will allow you to mindfully better utilize the values that are important to you and to quickly recognize how they can make a difficult situation less difficult and a good situation even better.

Our values play a pivotal role in our relationships and getting what we want out of life. Yet, conversations about values aren't held very often. When people are asked if they are successful, they tend to look at *what they have* to answer that question rather than *who they are* and *how they affect their sphere of the world and the people in it.* We seem to think that the keys to a great life are getting the best education money can buy, finding the right job, getting on the right career path, knowing the 'right' people and amassing bank accounts that will allow us to buy that nice home and outfit our garage with fine vehicles, to nicely clothe our 2.5 children that 'someone' has claimed to be the "ideal number," to travel, to dine out often, to do whatever we can to convey a picture of success. We have slapped a price tag on everything. We judge people by what we see on the outside. "He must be doing well" is no longer a statement of fact about someone's financial situation. We seem to think that those doing well must also be good people, smart people, business leaders or from good families–yet perhaps none of that is true. Money does play a role in our lives but our bank accounts are not a measurement of whether we are on the path to living our best life.

Take a moment and answer the following—honestly, of course.

Of the people who know you or with whom you have interacted within the last few months, would any of them have reason to consider you to be:

- unkind
- irresponsible
- dishonest
- impatient
- ungrateful
- rude
- insensitive
- careless
- intolerant
- disrespectful
- unfriendly?

Most people, if answering honestly, would probably have at least a few "yes" responses. That means there is room for improvement to optimize your life to be the best it can be. We can help you with that.

Now, think about how important the following things are to you. Are they *very important*, *somewhat important* or *not important?*
- Smiling
- Laughing
- Friends
- Family
- Children (if you have them)
- Pets (if you have them)

- Causes (e.g., the environment, animal organizations, political/social issues)
- Your Faith/Spirituality
- Hobbies

Now do the same with the following. How important is it to you to have the following things. Again, answer honestly. There are no right or wrong answers. No one is judging you here. Is it *very important, somewhat important* or *not important*?
- A big house.
- A nice car.
- A prestigious, well-paying job.
- A High-Def television.
- A computer.
- An iPod.
- Nice furniture.
- A vacation home.
- Designer or very nice clothing.
- The latest video game system (for you or your kids).

For many of us, the answers to both lists would contain many *very important* or *somewhat important* responses. That's fine. That's perfectly okay. What is important, however, is to understand the difference between what money can buy and what it can't. No one would dispute that being independently wealthy would be a fabulous thing to be—to have all that money could buy in terms of things you might need or want, or to be able to give generously to causes you believe in. How fabulous would that be? It would be great; however, most of us are not in that position.

The purpose of these lists is to show you that while we may consider many things in our life to be important on some level, there is a very distinct difference between them in terms of their value to us. Everything in the second list can be replaced. It has some sort of face value; it can be assessed in the financial world. The majority of the first list consists of what can only be considered priceless and irreplaceable. Would anyone lament the loss of an iPod in the same manner as a family pet or other loved one? *Keeping what is important to us in perspective* is another key element to getting the most out of a values-driven life.

One area where we are all equals, something that is true for all people—whether we have billions or not a cent to our name—is that the most valuable thing we can give someone is us. It is our most prized possession, if you will. What makes each of us so priceless is our values and the way we choose to practice them.

We each have the power to flourish, to succeed in every aspect of our life
when we:

- know what our values are.
- are mindfully aware of practicing them.
- optimize the way values work for us in our lives.

Couple the above values practice with keeping a balanced perspective on our material possessions relative to our inner dreams, and on what drives us to be who we are, and we are on our way to leading a values-driven life—our best life.

Chapter 2

Benefits to Living a Values-Driven Life

Now that we have a new understanding of the basic building blocks to start living a values-driven life, you might be wondering, "Why would I want or need to live this way?" In other words, "What do I get out of it?"

Well, the first thing to recognize is that our lives are basically all about relationships. It bears repeating: essentially, *life is all about relationships.*

- There is the very personal and perhaps most important relationship we have—with ourselves.
- There are our familial relationships, those we have with our spouses or significant others, with parents, children, and other relatives.
- There are our business relationships, the interactions we have with our bosses, coworkers, subordinates, clients, vendors, and other organizations.
- There are community relationships, sometimes these include close friendships, and sometimes they are more aloof or distant in nature. In our communities we interact with neighbors, school staff, clerks at local stores, garbage collectors, mail delivery persons, staff at the local gym or yoga studio, and the parents of our children's friends, classmates or teammates.
- Then there are old friends from high school, from college or from some other time in our life.
- And our pets. Pets are family members, too.

It's worth noting that not all meaningful relationships have to be with actual human beings. We can have strong relationships with sports teams, television shows and special causes. These commitments or interests are also important types of relationships in our lives.

Sometimes we have relationships for short periods of time—sort of temporary or fleeting interactions.

- We run in a 5K race (Amy) or in a marathon (Liz) and interact with other runners pre-, post- and during the race.
- We teach a class for a semester and develop a relationship with our students and sometimes their parents.
- We hire a painter or contractor to do work on our house and interact with this person(s) for the duration of the contract.
- We hire people who do regular, longer-term services for us: lawn care providers, housekeepers, dog walkers, babysitters.
- We attend concerts, go to the theater or have season tickets to sports events where we may strike up conversations with fellow ticket holders sharing opinions, commiserations or other observations we relate to because we are sharing the same experience or the same interest.

Liz loves the group camaraderie in marathons.

Day in and day out, our lives are all about these relationships. How we choose to behave in these relationships—that is to say, the values we practice and the way in which we practice them—can have a tremendous positive or negative impact on our lives. They can enhance our life or detract from it. They can improve our standing in the community or cause people to keep their distance. They can assist us when we are going for that promotion or put the proverbial nail in the coffin for our career advancement. They can win us friends or result in our making enemies. They can get us nicknames or labels like "mensch," "good egg," and "dependable" or "diva," "helicopter parent," "high-maintenance" and worse.

When we see a person act a certain way over and over, their behavior ends up defining them to some extent. There is a funny scene in the movie *Bridget Jones' Diary* where Bridget is told to include interesting facts about people when she introduces them. The scene shows what she might like to say (which is not so nice but what she really thinks) versus what she does say (which is polite). Think about how someone might introduce you. What do you think would be said? Would everyone who has interacted with you share this opinion? Do you feel that how you are viewed by others is an accurate picture of who you are or who you want to be? Our relationships with people and the consistency of our values practices does indeed paint a picture of who we are, and the people with whom we interact will perpetuate that view of us.

Now, it would be impossible to address every type of relationship we have and the complexities that may exist within those relationships. It is equally as impossible to address every benefit that can be achieved from living a values-driven life. We will, however, attempt to talk about many of the key relationships in our lives and touch upon others. We will also provide examples of the benefits that we gain from mindfully living a values-driven life. You will get the most benefit if, on your own, you use the tools and examples we give you here to look at all your relationships and all the goals you have within those relationships to identify the improvements and benefits that you can achieve by becoming more values-driven in how you live

I. Me, Myself and I

Let's start with, arguably, the most important relationship you have—your relationship with yourself. You might be wondering, is that really a relationship? Absolutely! If you don't have a good understanding of yourself, of who you are, then how can you possibly present your true self to others? How can you build honest, genuine relationships with others if you aren't even sure of who you are, what's important to you and what you like in yourself and others? Knowing yourself well is pretty essential wisdom. So, let's get started.

How do you feel about yourself most of the time?
Pretty big question, isn't it? Here are some questions to help you refine your answer:

- Do you respect yourself? Are you confident?
- Are you happy? What makes you happy? Who makes you happy?
- Is there love in your life? Whom or what do you love?

- Are you grateful? For what? For whom?
- Are you responsible? How do you exhibit this value?
- What are your five best traits?
- What are the five best traits of people you love, respect or care about?

As you answer these questions think about adding "why" to the end of each in order to further delve into your relationship with yourself. It's important to understand what "pushes your buttons" —in both a constructive and destructive way—so that you can get the most out of what lies on the positive side of the equation as you diminish the impact of the not-so-positive situations you may find yourself in.

We acknowledge the fact that we cannot always avoid doing or being exposed to undesirable things. So something constructive we can do for ourselves is to be prepared for whatever unpleasantness may come our way. We can prepare ourselves to keep our values from backsliding when negative situations crop up.

For example, rush hour traffic is a hassle and stressful and sometimes can't be avoided. What **can** be affected is how we react to this bother—do we let it get the best of us or do we find ways to minimize this nuisance without letting it move us to a place where those destructive values take hold and spill over into other aspects of our lives?

Now, daily rush hour traffic is pretty predictable, but it is impossible to forecast when other things will go awry. So isn't it, then, impossible to predict or plan for how we will react? Not really, so don't give into that notion. It is true that the majority of the time we have a spontaneous reaction to the little curve balls that get thrown at us, so a reasonable question would be, "How do we control gut reactions or on-the-spot decision-making?"

While you cannot always plan or know how you will act in a specific situation, you can plan and strive to behave a certain way under stressful situations. If you know you are prone to quickly get angry, become impatient or lash out verbally in an unkind manner when under pressure from difficult and unforeseen challenges, then you can simply decide to change that pattern. You can coach yourself into behaving differently by telling yourself what your ideal reaction would be. If you mindfully focus on who you want to be—including how you want to behave in various environments and situations—then you will be able to change. It may not happen right away. You might find yourself being your old, angry self the first time something goes wrong. The first step might be apologizing to yourself or to others, if appropriate, for that behavior. Admitting is often a first step to overcoming. Recognizing how your negative behavior makes you or others feel might be a look in the mirror that has a lasting impact. The point is, we should not accept that there are values or behaviors over which we have no control. That's not true, we just may have to retrain ourselves to act the way we want to act and be the person we want to be.

As with anything, reinforcement is the key. If we've always done things one way, it may be difficult to change but it's not impossible. Knowing yourself, being aware of what is important to you, what makes you feel good, what makes you feel badly, and doing a little dissection along the way will get your personal relationship with yourself on firmer ground, and all of your other relationships will benefit.

So, how well do you really know yourself? Do you know what values are the most important to you? The relationship you have with yourself takes care and feeding like any other relationship and you have to be able to recognize the red flags when things are not quite right. When you do the following things or behave the following ways, it may be an indication that your values need a little attention:

- You start missing appointments or showing up late. (**Accountability**)
- You snap at people or treat them unkindly. (**Civility**)
- You feel sad or begin looking at things negatively. (**Happiness**)
- You get angry or frustrated when things aren't going your way. (**Gratitude**)
- You look in the mirror and don't like what you see. (**Self-Respect**)
- You feel alone, or empty inside. (**Love**)

How does it benefit you to keep your values tuned up? The obvious answer is that it's way better to be happy than sad, to be in love than wanting, to be confident than unsure, to be appreciative than ungrateful, to be caring than unkind.

But perhaps an easier way to look at it is to show how it does not benefit you when you let your values practice slip. Keeping your values well-tuned can prevent any sort of negative domino effect from pummeling you over and over again. Let's look at just one seemingly inconsequential example of how your values practice can cost you dearly:

You act irresponsibly. → This causes others to feel slighted, upset or angry. → Others express those feelings to you, which may make you feel badly. → You choose not to acknowledge or apologize for your failing and are then viewed as uncivil or unkind as well as irresponsible. → Your behavior is shared with others. Your reputation is damaged and you will pay the consequence by potentially losing professional or personal standing amongst colleagues/friends. → This reputation damage can have future consequences with future career paths or with your being excluded socially or by groups/organizations of which you wish to be a part.

When we consistently practice our values in a constructive manner, there is a positive aura around us. If we are not doing things to upset ourselves or others or that are contrary to how we want to practice our values, then our lives are in balance; we are free of self-imposed conflicts. There are always challenges and conflicts in life, but we feel at peace knowing our behavior is not causing or contributing to any unpleasantness that may be going on around us. When we are unencumbered by self-imposed stresses, upsets or shortfalls, we can better address whatever challenges we face. This is tremendously beneficial—we are better fortified to deal with life and all that comes with it when we live our values in a positive manner.

II. Family

Now, let's take a look at our familial relationships. Families can be incredibly complex and confusing, incredibly loving and close, incredibly difficult and strange. They are not even necessarily similar, but we all belong to a family of some description or another.

We'd rather not define what a family means for you, but please take a moment and think of who is family to you. Is it your spouse and your kids? Your parents and siblings? Both? Is it a partner, a roommate, a boyfriend or girlfriend? Is it your dog and cat? Do you have step-parents or step-children? Or is your family some combination of all of those? Families come in all kinds of varieties—just think for a moment about who is family to you before you read on.

Brian, Amy, Claire and Chase make family vacations a priority.

Being part of a family means you are part of a group, and people who are part of a group are in a relationship, sometimes with many, many people, sometimes with just a few. When we are children we may view our family as our parents and our siblings. Our parents take care of us. They are our values teachers and mentors before we even know what that means. We look up to them and follow their lead. Our siblings can also be example setters or example followers or both. Siblings are sometimes the best of friends or not so much. We grow up managing these relationships, following rules, accepting consequences of breaking those rules and either growing closer to or farther apart from our siblings and parents as we mature, make outside friends, and follow our personal interests. There may be challenging times and wonderful, carefree times. All of these experiences leave their mark on us and have an impact on how we practice our values.

Family members have good relationships with one another when:

- they are honest with one another.
- they communicate openly.
- they are reliable.
- they are considerate of one another.
- they are tolerant of each other's differences.
- they play fair.
- they show respect for one another.
- they forgive each other for transgressions.

We don't get to pick our families, at least for the most part. We choose spouses or partners or adopt children, but the children born to us are who they are by luck of the draw, and we marry into families and inherit additional family members in that way. So while there is some choice, mostly there is little control over who we call family. Parents have been known to say "I love my kids all the time, but sometimes I don't like them very much." I am guessing many of us would say that about other family members—parents, siblings, cousins, or other relatives. That's what it's like in all relationships. There are good days and there are bad. The goal is to maximize the good and minimize the bad.

Family plays a major role in shaping our values, which makes sense considering how much time we spend with family. Parents teach children what's right and wrong and are the main models for them in terms of setting values examples. It is cringe-worthy when a parent says, "do as

I say and not as I do". Kids are much better at copying their parents' behaviors than they are at following their words when the two are at odds. A parent who frequently curses in front of his children should not be surprised to hear his child repeat his profane words, even if he has told them not to say what he says. A parent who is overheard telling a lie on the phone or being rude to someone is conveying a message that these things are okay to do. Where there are no consequences or admonishments imparted when siblings do not share, play fairly or treat one another with kindness, these behaviors are reinforced as acceptable and will be exhibited outside the home.

It's pretty simple; if you practice values in a not so positive manner in the presence of your children, you are all but saying these are acceptable values. Your children will go out into their worlds and emulate these same behaviors. As a result, you may end up with children who are having trouble making or keeping friends or who end up spending too much time in the principal's office. And like it or not, these seemingly tiny incidences follow children and grow—they develop reputations for being mean, rude, difficult or worse. In addition, one negative values practice by one child can quickly spread to other children as they, because of their immature and still developing brains, will often seek to respond to negative stimuli in an equally hurtful manner. It's quite possible that the parent may have inadvertently started it all by first setting the poor example and second by not pointing out to his child that the behavior he exhibited was not acceptable and should not be copied. Parents do make mistakes and need to admit to them, especially if a child is watching. Children are as good at forgiving parents as they are at copying them.

When we do not set or reinforce in others a positive values practice in our homes and with our families we end up with:

- stress
- discord
- arguments
- anger
- unhappiness
- confusion
- guilt
- self-esteem issues
- a lack of or an inability to trust.

And guess what? All of the above does not stay contained in your home and with your family. It spills over into other aspects of your life. If you are a child, you may carry it with you to school or onto the baseball field. It may interfere with your social interactions; it may interfere with your concentration and your ability to perform up to your ability in the classroom or on the playing field. If you are a parent, that stress will stay with you and you will be preoccupied. At work or in your community, the way you carry yourself, your mood, will be affected. You may be short with people, have trouble focusing and making your points clear, the quality of your work may suffer.

And it doesn't necessarily get any easier once our children are grown. In fact, it can be more difficult. Once children grow up, move out and establish families of their own, we end up with different types of relationships and it can be very challenging. Our values practice, however, remains critically important.

When your child marries, they now have another family to consider. All of a sudden there are decisions to make, like where to spend Thanksgiving, that haven't had to be made before. Feelings are at stake. It used to be easy—kids were with their parents, but now those kids may be married, have their own homes and maybe a set of in-laws. Scheduling special occasions is difficult and getting everyone to be in the same place at the same time is no longer an easy task. It can be a recipe for hurt feelings or an opportunity to bring out the best in everyone.

We've all heard the horror stories of families split apart over feeling slighted. All of a sudden, mature adults are acting like spoiled brats when they don't get their way. Someone doesn't come to Christmas dinner and the next thing you know they are banished from any future dinners. As we age and our extended families become bigger, it is ever so important to be able to adapt to the changes that come with that. We may have to bend a little bit and celebrate a birthday not on the actual date of someone's birth. We may have to adjust our expectation levels. We may have to relearn to be grateful for what we do have versus dwell on what we don't.

When we have been accustomed to the same tradition for many years, it may be difficult to give it up or to carry it on without all the usual suspects in attendance, but it behooves us to adapt and try to work out compromises or schedules everyone can agree to. Families transition, and how we adapt to those transitions is critical to keeping the peace.

Extended family summer beach gatherings were a tradition when we were young, but now it's more challenging to coordinate schedules to get everyone together.

When families are communicating, treating each other respectfully, being open, honest, tolerant and expressing their gratitude and love for one another, you will find yourself:

- happier
- more confident
- less stressed
- better able to concentrate
- more socially adept
- quicker to react and adapt to challenges
- smiling more
- laughing more
- more appreciative.

Families can be very complex, no doubt about it. Not everyone has supportive or even caring parents. Some families are dysfunctional. These are sad and unfortunate situations but they needn't be permanent states. Nor does the cycle of dysfunction need to continue, although it is indeed difficult to break. Every family has a little dysfunction at times. The teen years can be trying. Divorce can take quite a toll on families. Illnesses, absentee mothers or fathers, emotional or physical dependencies, disabilities and economic issues can all play a role in how well a family functions.

Regardless of the state of your family relations, the one thing that can keep things running smoothly or improve them is the way in which you practice your values. If your family life is not so great, you can make it better by choosing to be more respectful and civil to one another; by being more tolerant and patient; by taking responsibility; by showing appreciation. Sometimes we do this by not saying a word; by biting our tongue rather than letting the negative words spew out. There are ups and downs in every family, sometimes daily!

When asked what comes first in life, the majority of people answer "family." Family is, in some ways, the center of our universe when it comes to reinforcing the practice of positive values. The negative and positive that we learn, that we practice in that core will emanate out from there impacting the rest of our universe accordingly. This can be beneficial to other areas of our life or not. "Family values" are not always good. It's important to recognize and reinforce the good, and to recognize and reject the bad.

We may not always be able to choose who our families are, but we can choose how we behave and interact with them. Everyone likes to be included. The family is one group where you should always feel loved, accepted and appreciated. If you have this, then you have an invaluable support network that can help you improve and enrich other important relationships in your life.

III. At the Office

Work is a significant part of our lives. Our livelihood is dependent upon our jobs and how well we perform them. It would reason, then, that our work or business relationships are quite important to our well-being. When it comes to understanding how our values practice benefits us at work, it seems rather easy. If we practice positive values, we keep our jobs and put ourselves on the path to a promotion. If we practice negative values, then we may get fired or stagnate in the same position. In general, this is true, but there is more to it than that. It isn't just about keeping our job, although that is a pretty crucial need for most working people.

If you work, let's start with asking yourself why you work. And let's take a very broad definition of work here. For example, stay-at-home parents are, for all intents and purposes, working. Their job may be to clean house, do laundry, run errands, take care of children, manage services to be done on their homes/things they own and keep things moving smoothly, in general. A paycheck need not be earned for you to work. So, why do you work? Think about ALL the reasons. There are usually many reasons why we choose to work. The main drivers for why we work can normally be categorized as financial, psychological/emotional, or intellectual.

Financial reasons may include:

- The need for income to meet financial requirements.
- The want of income for discretionary spending—for wishes like travel and high-definition television sets.
- The want of income to save for kids' college tuition or to retire sooner.
- To have peace of mind that additional income brings; financial security.

Psychological/emotional reasons may include:

- Altruistic reasons—a desire to simply do good with your work.
- Interest in a particular cause.
- A need or desire to contribute to society or the economy.
- Strong ambition to succeed in business or a particular line of work.
- Enjoying being a leader.
- Enjoying working towards a goal as part of a team.
- To feel like a financial contributor in your household; a self-worth need.

Intellectual reasons may include:

- Interest in/desire to put education to use.
- Interest in contributing to the advancement of something, such as scientific cures or technological advances.
- Desire to create or invent.
- A need or desire to continue learning.
- A need or desire to share your knowledge with others.
- To feel fulfilled or challenged intellectually.

There are reasons why we work and why we choose the jobs or career paths that we do. What we get out of our work can vary, but we all have the same capacity to excel in our jobs and in our work relationships. Whether we work at a fast food restaurant or run a corporation, we interact with coworkers, clients, vendors and others. We connect with people in person, via phone, email and text. We often work within close proximity of others—our coworkers and/or our customers. These relationships at "the office" and the way that we choose to behave and exist within them are quite important. From these relationships managers, coworkers and others will decide whether you are:

- a team player or out for yourself.
- responsible with meeting deadlines or unreliable.
- confident in your abilities or unsure of yourself.
- civil and approachable or discourteous and aloof.
- ambitious or indifferent.
- an achiever or unmotivated.
- likable or difficult.

All of the above, along with other traits you exhibit in your workplace, come to define your character, who you are. These things will also play into how successful you are in your job. If you are viewed as difficult, aloof, unreliable then aside from worrying about being able to keep your job, you might be passed over for promotions or other positions for which you are qualified. Your performance on the job, which includes your values practices, can make or break you.

Your reputation is important. Period. As they say, it precedes you. Got a good one? Congratulations! Got a bad one? Then you've got quite a hole to climb out of. In your place of work your reputation can either help pave the way for you or be a roadblock. It's pretty easy to understand that if you enjoy a reputation of being reliable, confident, capable, approachable, easy to work with and ambitious you can expect:

- to keep your job.
- to receive regular pay increases.
- to be recommended for bonuses.
- to be recommended for promotions/other positions.
- to be respected by your peers and superiors.
- to receive positive referrals/recommendations from those who know you.
- for people to want to do business with you.
- to be viewed as a leader, as an example to follow.
- to be successful in your job.

Now let's look at what happens when you choose to be irresponsible, lackadaisical, wishy-washy, difficult to work with, rude or short with people, and untrustworthy. If you exhibit these traits or practice the values associated with them you can expect:

- to have no job security. You will be viewed as expendable.
- to be disrespected by your peers and supervisors.
- to not be trusted.
- to not be given opportunities to lead.
- to be avoided by your coworkers.
- to be reprimanded by human resources.
- to cost your employer business.
- to stagnate in your position.
- to not be empowered.

In short, you increase your chances of having job security and a career path if you choose to practice positive values on the job. Not only are you adding to your skills and experience résumé with each and every job that you hold, your values résumé continues to be updated along the way, too. That résumé is sometimes as or more important that the one that conveys your education and job experience. Many people look good "on paper" but the proof is in the pudding. There may be many people who are qualified for a given position so the differentiators may be how you present yourself and what others say about you:

Positive values on the job play into what future opportunities you have.

- Do you come across as trustworthy?
- Do you seem to interact well with others—are you civil, friendly, open?
- Do your references consider you to be:
    - reliable and accountable?
    - a leader?
    - a person of integrity?
    - driven?
    - someone who works well with others?

Our values can be key differentiators for us when it comes to work—with getting a job, keeping it and/or moving up the proverbial corporate ladder.

These are just a few of the work-related benefits, but just about everyone takes a little work home with them. Either literally or figuratively we carry work outside of the office. How do you think it impacts our home life if our work environment is one where the people there:

- get along?
- support one another?
- are civil to one another?
- take personal responsibility?
- care about their individual performance and its impact on others?
- care about the success of their peers and the organization as a whole?
- think before they press the send button?
- respect one another?
- are confident in themselves and the work they do?
- are happy to be there?
- love their job or are working for ones they love?

It would reason that if you worked in such an environment, and that if you contributed to generating a positive atmosphere, then the positive would follow you out the door. You'd arrive home with less stress and in a better mood than if you worked in an environment where people:

- complained and griped about their jobs.
- only cared about earning a paycheck.
- were not willing to go the extra mile for a coworker, a team or the organization.
- hated or were indifferent about their jobs.
- said what was on their minds regardless of whether

it was civil or kind.
- played the victim or blamed others rather than were accountable.
- could not be trusted.
- were unhappy or exuded a dissatisfaction with being at work.
- didn't show respect or tolerance for others.

It is a fact that the quality of and the types of interactions we have within our office relationships spill over into our lives outside of work. Have you ever met a friend for coffee and knew right away something was wrong? They were not smiling maybe, were distracted or were short with you? Then you come to find out something is amiss at work. Maybe someone is being rude, making things difficult, or saying untrue things. You may end up spending your entire coffee break talking about this work issue. That's what friends are for, of course, but wouldn't most of us choose to talk about more positive things going on in our lives? That trip we just took, or our children, or a book we recently read?

When our jobs are bringing us down, when things are not right at work, outside of work we are more likely to:

- be unhappy.
- be curt with our spouses, partners or children.
- lose confidence in our abilities.
- worry.
- lose sleep.
- complain.
- be less fun to be around.
- turn inward and away from others.
- lose patience quickly.
- get angry quickly.

- become depressed.

Work is a significant part of our lives. It contributes considerably if not exclusively to our financial well-being. Money can be the cause of all kinds of stress. We worry about making enough, about how to make more, about what to do with what we make. Finances are important and will never, for the most part, be something we do not think about, but wouldn't it be nice if we didn't have to stress about anything else related to our jobs? Or at least minimally stress about them? The one and perhaps only way to do this is to ensure that our values drive our behavior and performance at the office. If we have to be at work, and most of us have to work, then shouldn't we do whatever we can to make the most of that part of our lives? To enjoy it as best we can while we're there and not allow it to create unnecessary stress in other areas of our lives? Most people go to work five days a week—sometimes more—our values practice choices at work, then, have a daily impact on our lives. This is huge. It is worth our values investment.

IV. Community

In your community you do all sorts of things: grocery shop, mail packages, work out at the gym, go to school, frequent coffee shops, eat at restaurants, see movies, attend sporting events, go to the pool, shop at the mall, attend religious services, and help out in your child's classroom. This is a short list meant to represent how we spend our time when not at home or at work.

Wherever we go and whatever we do, we all interact with other people. If we drive someplace, we share the road with fellow travelers. When we get to our destination, we share that space with whoever happens to be there at the same time. If we're doing some sort of shopping we are exchanging monies, and perhaps pleasantries, with a salesperson. We are navigating parking lots and grocery store aisles, waiting in line for our turn, making purchases or exchanges. We are relating, if even in a small, seemingly insignificant way, with other people. We are part of the lives of strangers, at times, for mere moments sharing a smile, a nod, a "thank you" or an "excuse me."

When we interact and connect with our neighbors, we build a positive sense of community.

But these relationships aren't as important and don't affect us the same way as our family or work relationships do, right? Well...think again. Has anyone—any stranger or person you don't know well—ever ruined your day or at least given it a "black eye" by being rude, unkind, selfish, offensive, hurtful, ungrateful or self-righteous towards or with you? When these things happen, our feelings get hurt or maybe we get angry, and these feelings sometimes stay with us, affecting us in those other parts of our universe.

Sometimes negative comments can shake our confidence for a moment or even make a more lasting impression. Words are very powerful, even when coming from complete strangers. Derisive looks can also pack a wallop. We all have opinions about many, many things. If we all, however, shared what we were thinking every moment we were thinking it, then we'd likely alienate a lot of people. All of our thoughts are not always friendly or positive ones. We can't always control our thoughts but we can control our words, our reactions, our gestures.

Living in communities takes a lot of patience, tolerance and understanding. We ALL have grocery shopping to do and packages to mail. Lines can get long. Registers can fail. People can get impatient. What shapes our communities is the people who live in them. When gang members are infiltrating neighborhoods, residents rise up to get them out. Why? Because they can create a negative backlash for the community as a whole. They may threaten the safety of the neighborhood, they may be disrespectful to women or other groups. They may prevent people from enjoying their parks or chatting with a friend on the front stoop. It doesn't take a gang, however, to cause a community to feel unfriendly.

What types of behaviors can be a detriment to communities? What types of poor values practices threaten our communities in ways that make us dread having to go out? Have you ever seen the following occur?

- Someone having a cell phone conversation during a

lunch with another or during a shopping transaction with a clerk?
- Someone passing through a door and not holding it open for the person behind to pass through?
- Someone angrily and/or disrespectfully blaming a cashier for a long line or a computer glitch?
- Someone cutting someone else off in traffic?
- Someone expressing their frustration to another with not-so-nice hand gestures?
- Someone blaming a teacher or a school for a child's less than stellar academic performance?
- Someone standing up at a PTA meeting and expressing an opinion in a rude and accusatory manner?
- Someone ignoring or failing to acknowledge you as they pass on the sidewalk?

These are common types of uncivil behaviors that we see, and if they occur often enough they will begin to define our communities.

When too many people seem not to care or seem to be careless in their actions and behaviors, others may follow suit. That "why should I care" feeling will creep out in response to seeing others not care.

- We see it in neighborhoods—people stop tending to their homes, paint starts to peel, wood starts to rot, lawns become overgrown or die. What is the consequence? The values of our homes go down. Some people move if it can't be stopped, but others fall in line and accept that lower standard.
- We see it at places of business. The pleasant, friendly coffee barista becomes much quieter the more she says hello to customers who continue

to answer her with silence. The grocery store clerk who has been chided by too many impatient customers will begin to hurry through your order no longer looking you in the eye, offering you a smile or asking how you're doing today.
- We see it on the roads we regularly travel. Getting cut off in traffic one too many times can cause other drivers to become more aggressive or less civil. People failing to yield to pedestrians crossing the street causes upset and danger.
- We see it on our sidewalks. Community members who keep their heads down as they walk past sending the message that they do not want to talk to you. This causes discomfort and can result in people avoiding eye contact and conversations in general when meeting and passing others for fear their friendly overtures are imposing or unwanted.

The impact of these seemingly small slights or inconsequential actions can, indeed, have consequences on communities as a whole. It becomes less pleasant to be out and about in your community. You begin to dread when you must navigate in a world that you view to be unfriendly. Rather than being part of your day that could bring an opportunity to meet others you know in passing or result in the exchange of a cute or interesting story, errands are considered successful if you didn't have some sort of negative run-in with anyone. That is not the kind of community most of us want to live in.

Most of us want to feel that our communities are safe, that the businesses are staffed with knowledgeable, good people and that the people we'll run into as we go about our lives are much like us and, as such, are trying to make a positive impact on the community. We want our schools and our children's teachers to be welcoming to us, to see us as members of the same team working for what's best for our children. We want business owners to see us as good customers and we want to do business with companies that treat us that way.

Our communities are reflections of the people who live in them and work in them. When we choose to put our values first in the way we function, we are helping to define and shape our community. If honesty, kindness, gratitude, respect and tolerance are widely practiced in a community, it makes it a better place to live.

When we think of communities, we tend to think of houses, places of business, fire stations, post offices, parks, libraries, shopping and dining venues. These are all places that make up communities, but what gives communities their character are their people. A town is not gossipy—people are. A town is not seedy unto itself—people and their actions make it that way. A park is not dangerous—it's the people who frequent it who would make it so. Neglect causes things to fall into states of disrepair. When we neglect our values the same thing happens. It affects us and others, like our communities. When poor values choices are made *en masse,* communities suffer severe consequences—they become places where people are unhappy, feel trapped and where they no longer want to live.

V. Friends

Friends are a unique class of relationship that deserves its own special attention. Friendship means different things to different people. What you consider to be the definition of friendship might be different than what your best friend thinks.

The <u>Stanford Encyclopedia of Philosophy</u> defines friendship in this way: *"Friendship, as understood here, is a distinctively personal relationship that is grounded in a concern on the part of each friend for the welfare of the other, for the other's sake, and that involves some degree of intimacy. As such, friendship is undoubtedly central to our lives, in part because the special concern we have for our friends must have a place within a broader set of concerns, including moral concerns, and in part because our friends can help shape who we are as persons."*

This definition seems to underscore how important and influential our friendships can be. We've all heard the phrase, "you will be judged by the company you keep." Parents love to throw that line out there when their kids begin hanging out with the "wrong crowd." Right or wrong, however, it is true. If you spend time with someone known for being a certain way—dishonest, criminal, hateful—people will assume you

Shared athletic activities can be a great way to establish friendships.

share those same values or traits. It may seem like guilt by association, but don't we often seek to make friends or acquaintances with others who share our interests, beliefs, sense of humor or outlook on life? We do. So while being judged by the company we keep may seem unfair, it has been proven that we share many similarities with the people with whom we choose to spend our time. The phrase "choose your friends wisely" seems like rather good advice now, doesn't it?

There is no doubt that our friends help shape who we are as people and that we help shape our friends in the same way. Peer pressure reigns in friendships. When you care about someone enough to call them a friend you are more forgiving of their transgressions than you would be of an acquaintance. You cherish your relationship, so you are willing to go out of your way to help, to show you care, to ease their burden. Showing a friend kindness, love, gratitude and respect is a true gift that results in a mutual happiness. There are many ways in which we let friends know they are friends:

- We keep in touch with them.
- We talk.
- We share.
- We listen.
- We laugh.
- We commiserate.
- We grieve.
- We empathize.

When we do these things we are being good friends.

Now, friendships can have their low points, too. Sometimes we take friends for granted. They are our friends, so we know they will forgive us. This isn't okay but probably forgivable if it is the exception rather than the rule. Friends, however, who don't show up on time or at all when they say they will, forget to call or email, are distracted or unsupportive are not very good friends. Friends, sometimes, will even ask too much of one another and then things get complicated.

- What if a friend tells you s/he did something illegal? Are you supposed to keep that secret?
- What if your friend asks you to do something that you think is unethical or that you are uncomfortable doing?
- What if there are things about your friend that you don't like—what then?

A good friend doesn't ask you or expect you to do anything you don't want to do or that is illegal or unethical. Being a good friend, however, may make you feel like you should do those things even if you don't want to. When we care about someone we don't like to let them down. We may try to trivialize the issue into not being as "big" as it may seem. We may tell ourselves we owe it to our friend because we've shared such a special friendship. But don't our friends owe it to us not to put us in such a position?

The point is, we sometimes do things for friends that we might not otherwise want to do; we might put aside our values in order to agree to a friend's request. Sometimes peer pressure is more overt—the prodding to have another drink, to change someone's "no" to a "yes". Other times it's not so obvious. We want to please people who are our friends, we want to keep things moving along nice and smoothly so when requests are made—to keep a secret, to have another drink, to go to a movie you don't want to see, or to do something that is against your values—we want to say "yes" because the request is coming from a friend. We think this is how we show our friendship, our loyalty, our trust.

Unlike life partners, friendships can be founded upon a small, singular connection with someone. Perhaps we share a common interest and our friendship is centered around that—biking or running or knitting or reading. Some people have book club friends or running buddies. Sometimes people are brought together by their kids and their interests. Other times, friends become very close and vacation together or regularly schedule get-togethers—the bond in these close friendships is a kind of love, there is a greater attachment. Whatever the level of friendship, our friends influence us and we them. We may parent differently after we are exposed to the parenting skills of a friend. We may change our eating habits, we may start exercising more, watch new television shows, listen to different music, travel to far off destinations or read certain books all because a friend, someone we like and who we respect, recommended them.

So if we can do all of these things just because a friend asks us to or recommends them or does these things herself, then couldn't we find ourselves going against our values for a friend? Supporting or keeping silent when a friend makes a poor choice? Going along with something that we don't believe in because your friend wants us to? It's a slippery slope. Silence is acceptance. If we don't speak up, we cannot not expect someone to change. And if we keep not speaking up, we may begin to think whatever the objectionable behavior is—being ungrateful, rude, unkind, unethical or dishonest—is not that big a deal anymore. We might even find ourselves letting our values slip and acting that way. Friendships are very powerful influences. If we feed and care for our friendships, we can benefit by:

- growing from the knowledge and experience of our friend.
- enjoying additional and diverse social interactions.
- having people who share our interests to do things with.
- having a supportive person to turn to for advice or help in challenging times.
- having someone just to talk to; someone whose company we enjoy.
- feeling fulfilled, connected or included versus lonely or wanting.

VI. The Value of Values

No matter what we do in our lives, we are building connections with others and ourselves. The kinds of relationships and interactions we have with family, friends, co-workers, relatives, lovers, community members and people we meet in passing often define whether it's a good day or a bad one; a happy life or one that could use a few more smiles and a little more laughter in it. When we strive to live a values-driven life, to bring positive values practices into our relationships, we see the many benefits that can be achieved—no matter which relationship we're speaking of. There are personal benefits and relationship benefits.

Being values-driven increases our capacity for:

- happiness
- productivity
- creativity
- focus
- communication
- patience
- respect
- civility
- gratitude
- love
- responsibility.

The effects of this on our various relationships can be seen in the following ways:

- less stress at home and overall
- improved health
- a more active social life
- a more intimate relationship with a spouse or significant other
- happier, more confident children
- an overall feeling of being fulfilled or at peace
- career success
- improved financial station
- being viewed as a positive role model
- feeling wanted or needed and making others feel the same.

Our lives are, at their core, all about relationships. Through our values practice we have the ability to strengthen all of our relationships and forge new, meaningful ones that not only benefit us but everyone else as well. When we are not aligned with our values, or we are not practicing positive values, we end up with internal conflict and our relationships can become destructive. And that benefits no one.

Chapter 3

The Core Five—Our Five-to-Be-Alive Values

Values. Now that we have a better sense of them and the benefits to living in alignment with our values, we want to take a cookie break!

In our worlds, cookies go well with most occasions. But here we want to visualize life as a yummy AND healthy cookie and what goes into creating such a nutritious confection. Now, if props would be helpful to you, absolutely enjoy a cookie (or two) as you read!

As you may be starting to gather, there are more values than we can cover in one book. They are a very individual mix. Even though we are the Values Gals, our values do not match identically, nor are they likely to precisely match your values. We may share many of the same ones, but they might be in different orders of importance. We may even be wildly different in our values. But as we've been discussing, there are core values that are likely to be on everyone's list.

What we have observed is that, among people's core values, there are five that are universally important as the key ingredients to creating and sustaining our best possible lives. Like most of you, we have negotiated some fairly daunting life challenges. Practicing our core values has been and continues to be the key to meeting those challenges successfully and designing lives that we didn't dare dream of years ago. These five values are the difference between failing to reach our goals and, not only honoring our commitments to ourselves, but going beyond our own expectations... and not regressing to our original habits.

For example, how many times have you decided to drop a few pounds? Or perhaps you've started significant weight loss programs? And maybe you made your goals and felt fantastic.

- How long did you stay at your goal weight?
- How many times have you put the weight back on and had to start the weight loss routine all over again?

It's exhausting isn't it? It's frustrating—it takes time and energy, and it can be a real stressor to our self-image, which then can have a domino effect on our feelings of self-confidence, self-worth and happiness, which, in turn, negatively affects our relationships, our work, and our health.

These five cornerstone values make the difference in our lives between:

- being healthy and happy and living our dreams, or
- being stressed, depressed and feeling stuck in a rut with our dreams out of reach.

Which life do you choose to live?

Our Best-Life Design? A Cookie

Now, let's get back to our cookie comparison. If you look at your life as a cookie, what kind of cookie is it?

- Is it loaded with nuggets of tasty, gooey and crunchy treasures? Or is it more crumbly, unsatisfying and bland?
- Is your life cookie made with quality, natural, wholesome ingredients? Or is your cookie chock full of chemicalized ingredients that you can't pronounce and aren't really sure whether they are genuine food?
- Is this a cookie that you can't wait to taste or is it relatively tasteless, leaving you empty and wanting something else?

Life, like a yummy cookie, is a treasure, and we all deserve to experience the best of both—like cookies, life should be bursting with amazing flavors and textures, being both good and good for us.

So how do we make the best lives for ourselves? The same way we make the best cookies—with the essential quality ingredients.

The Five-to-Be-Alive values are the five cornerstone values that have the power to lead each of us to:

- **designing**,
- **achieving**, and
- **maintaining** our best possible lives.

If we set any goal or begin following any dream, no matter how miniscule or grandiose, by starting with these five ingredients in our action plan, we can end up with results beyond our imagining.

Five-to-Be-Alive values are the basics—the foundation of our values system for any specific situation and for our overall quality of life. Daily attention to and alignment with the Five-to-Be-Alive values will guide us to make significant, positive, lasting shifts in our immediate goals and, ultimately, our lives.

What are the Five-to-Be-Alive Values?

The Five-to-Be-Alive values are our keys or building blocks for lasting life changes, our ingredients for our best and most balanced lives. And they are:

- **Accountability**
- **Self-Respect**
- **Love**
- **Happiness**, and,
- (thank you very much), **Gratitude**.

We take an in-depth look at each of these values in the following pages. But let's talk big picture here for a minute. Just as with baking, each of the five values or *ingredients* is necessary for us to get the *recipe* right. Baking is an equation—we must blend a certain balance of fat, eggs, leavening, flour, and sugar before we can create a successful cookie. If we forget an ingredient, we end up with something that resembles a cookie but isn't quite there. If we leave out the leavening, we likely end up with very flat, thin, and potentially burned cookie-like discs. Likewise, if we neglect to include self-respect in our daily values practice, we will fall short of our goals or of being able to maintain them.

Additionally, the Five-to-Be-Alive values are not interchangeable with other values that we may practice or are part of our values system. Of course, other values factor in to most situations we seek to improve. Those supplemental values are more akin to cookie variations or flavorings—like chocolate chips or cinnamon or walnuts—than to the basic cookie building blocks. For example, if we try to substitute oil for eggs (which don't serve the same function in baking), we risk runny, doughy results that never really resemble a cookie.

We call these five core values the Five-to-Be-Alive values because these five, when practiced consciously and consistently, are universally vital to living our sweetest, happiest, most productive and constructive lives.

Ready to come alive? Let's get to the heart of our values systems!

Accountability

The Basics
When we make a choice, take an action, utter a statement, accountability is being able to answer for our behavior. Can we and do we stand up for what we do? Do we follow through on taking the necessary steps to meet goals we set, fulfill promises we make, and achieve our life's dreams?

The buck stops with us—that's accountability. When we are accountable, we don't blame our choices and outcomes on others or circumstances, even though they may indeed be influencing factors. Ultimately, *we* decide and *we* are responsible for how *we* behave, whether *we* uphold our commitments to ourselves and to others, and whether *we* achieve the goals that are most important to us.

Inherent in this concept is the assumption that we will face challenges; we will be tested. Accountability plays into the design of our best lives in how we navigate those challenges:

- Do we do manage them in a way we can be proud of?
- Would our children, spouses, colleagues, family and friends respect how we handled a situation?
- Perhaps more importantly, are we proud of our own behavior?
- Do we honor our commitments, or do we end up looking like we make empty promises and set meaningless goals we had no intention of making or keeping?
- Asked another way, are we a person of our word and a person of integrity? Or are we a person who should not be believed, trusted or relied upon to do what we say we will or to do the right thing?

We are giving you lots of questions to consider. Here are the two most critical to ask ourselves in order for us to start living our best lives:

- **Which kind of person do I want to be?**
- **Which kind of person am I?**

These two questions are worth generous consideration, and we will come back to them for an in-depth exploration, for their answers carry importance beyond the topic of accountability. In the following chapters we will assess where we are in our practice of each of the Five-to-Be-Alive values and we will offer ways to customize strategies to get back in alignment and fine-tune our alignment with each of the five. Right now we want to focus on really understanding accountability as a value and why practicing accountability brings life-altering positive results.

Alignment

Accountability plays into almost every aspect of our day. We may not think of our behaviors as accountability tests, but to use a portion of my day as an example, from the moment I get out of bed in the morning to the time I set my alarm at night, each action in between is a barometer of my accountability.

Accountability gets me out the door most mornings on my run.

To better illustrate this exercise, let's breeze through an extremely abbreviated itemization of a recent typical morning:

- 5 out of 7 mornings a week I get up before sunrise and run before breakfast because, at the time of this writing, I'm training for a marathon that I am running as a charity fundraiser. When I'm not in training, I still run regularly to stay active, healthy,

happy, and in good shape.
- When I come back from each run, I walk my dog for 45 minutes so she can get her big exercise and exploration adventure for the day and start her day healthily and happily.
- When we return from our walk, I brush my dog and sweep and straighten my loft to keep a clean and tidy living and work space.
- After I feed my pup, I eat a healthy breakfast of egg whites and then a banana and almond butter smoothie, along with my vitamins and supplements.
- After showering, I address any emails that need replies, check the headlines for the morning, and start on whatever work project I am tasked with that day—usually either writing, photography or producing. This takes me through lunch.

Can you pick out my accountability in each of those actions? It's probably evident that I am committed to being physically fit, training healthily for a marathon, eating nutritiously, generally maintaining good health, being a responsible pack leader to my dog, keeping a healthy home, and being productive creatively and professionally. If my actions echo my commitments, then I am in alignment with accountability and well on my way to living the kind of life I dream about, achieving the benchmarks that are important to me and enjoying the process.

Granted, we are not Stepford people and we do not always do everything the way we want to or plan to. Sometimes, I may postpone work for errands or other commitments. Or maybe I'm exhausted and give myself an unplanned day off from running. There are days when

I'm just spent—the well feels dry creatively and I know it's time for a day to recharge my batteries—a day off from routine. Life is about balance, after all. Flexibility helps us keep our life in balance without slacking on our accountability.

In these examples, I am reshuffling my commitments, not abandoning them. If I stopped running altogether, or reduced my training to 3 days a week, it would be fair to say I would fall abysmally short of my goal to successfully run a marathon. And if I didn't curtail my calorie intake accordingly, I would be abdicating my commitment to being physically fit. And when the well is dry—my work suffers if I am not creatively charged. I could slog through an assignment tired and uninspired but it would take longer and be a shell of what it could be if I honored my process and took time away from a project to reinvigorate my creative juices.

Does it make sense now how our seemingly insignificant actions and choices throughout the day are deceptively tiny accountability measures that add up to a life-size scale? We either are in alignment with achieving the goals we've set for ourselves and in living the kind of life we want to live, or we are out of alignment with our accountability.

There is also the phenomenon of situational accountability. It might be obvious and easy to pledge allegiance to the bigger commitments we make. If we promise to deliver a project for work on time and on budget, that's a biggie and we work to make that happen. If we promise we will go home for the holidays, also a biggie and we follow through. If we resolve to get our high cholesterol under control, we take the necessary steps.

Knowing the potential consequences of not following through on the big stuff often keeps us on track.

But what about the little promises we make? When we say we're going to meet someone at a certain time, and yet we are consistently 10-15 minutes later than we say we will be, how does that reflect on our accountability? Is that really a question of accountability? We might think it's such a minor thing that it doesn't count. But we aren't the person who is consistently waiting for us. It's not minor when someone else manages to routinely be on time—despite traffic delays that they factored in when planning their transit time—and we are routinely late. Accountable is accountable. There aren't gradations of accountable. Routinely showing up on time and routinely showing up late are not the same thing.

If we are occasionally out of accountability alignment with ourselves, is that really such a big deal? Simply, it's a slippery slope. Once we start intentionally deviating, it's easier and easier to get farther away from our core value than we ever imagined.

Of course, we will encounter situations where we will do everything in our power to make good on our commitments and yet we fall short. But the key here is we gave it our all. We are consistently diligent about being accountable.

Let's take a minute to envision that slippery slope. Let's say I decide one morning that I need to lose some weight and that no matter what, I am *not* going to eat the chocolate bar stashed in my kitchen cabinet. Great. Now all I'm thinking about is that chocolate bar. So, after a successful morning of avoiding the chocolate bar, I have a couple squares from it around lunchtime thinking everything is fine in moderation, and put it away. Except, it was really tasty. And it's hard being on a diet without indulging in a reward now and then. So a couple squares more won't hurt. And then a bit later that day, I think well, it's really just a couple squares more to finish the bar so I won't be tempted by it tomorrow. By the end of the day, if not before, that chocolate bar is totally consumed. My accountability to myself, totally shot.

Do you think that leaves me with a positive feeling about myself? Or about my ability to do right by myself in other areas? If I'm feeling weak or small because I let a chocolate bar keep me from my eating plan, imagine how I'm going to feel when I'm faced with the next chocolate bar—literal or metaphoric.

Why Accountability?

Accountability is a cornerstone value in our Five-to-Be-Alive system because it is one of the key ingredients providing our fortitude, our ability to go the distance. When we set our sights on a goal we want to achieve or a life dream we aspire to, taking the steps necessary to get from where we are to where we want to be requires us to be responsible. We are accountable for making the choices and acting in ways that will get us there. And accountability is an essential part of that success recipe. Just like if we don't include the eggs in our cookie dough, we won't end up with the cookie we wanted.

When we are accountable:

- We follow through on our commitments.
- People see us as dependable.

- We will have a higher success rate at achieving goals and may be recognized and rewarded for that... at work, at home, in community, etc.
- Children trust us, as do adults.
- We approach goals with confidence and a can-do attitude.
- This aspect of our self-image is positive—we feel we can depend on ourselves.

If we start letting our accountability slide and get lazy and lax about our commitments to ourselves and others, we behave more and more in ways that are foreign to who we truly are and how we want to be. And when we are in discord with ourselves, when we are behaving counter to a value that is vitally important to us, we are:

- confused,
- upset,
- unhappy,
- stressed,
- even physically sick... and we might not understand why.

Once we start abandoning our accountability:

- Our friends, family and colleagues learn not to believe our promises.
- People who have observed us renege on our commitments do not trust us.
- We don't trust ourselves.
- Our self-image suffers, since we know we look for ways out of commitments and goals instead of ways to achieve them.
- Our personal and professional success rate suffers, in relationships and responsibilities.

- We don't achieve our goals consistently. We may even stop setting goals altogether.
- Unfinished projects will accumulate around us, contributing to our feelings of not living up to who we want to be.
- We are definitely NOT living the life of our dreams.

Self-Respect

The Basics
Self-respect is an internal conversation, yet it manifests externally. It is essentially a question of whether or not we like ourselves.

Self-esteem is another descriptor for this value. We often categorize others as having self-esteem—exhibiting confidence, a sense of security and assuredness—or low self-esteem—being insecure, afraid, shy, having low self-confidence, and shrinking from involvement. But we aren't concerned with what kind of self-esteem others may have. What matters is our own self-respect.

Self-respect is something we are all born with. We can lose it bit by bit along the way. And here's the kicker: we lose our self-respect solely through choices we make. No one can take our self-respect away from us. We hold our heads high, we walk with confidence, we feel we are being the best person we can be when we make the choices that are right for us.

Can you see where this is going? When we are in alignment with our core values, when we live in accord with the values that are important to us, we live with self-respect.

Alignment
Our self-respect affects our actions. While it is an internal feeling, it shows in how we carry ourselves, how we act, the choices we make, and the kind of life we lead and allow ourselves to dream about.

It helps me to understand something to paint a mental

picture. So let's see what it looks like when we are out of alignment with our self-respect. When we are running low on self-esteem or have little respect for ourselves, we:

- Physically slump and appear smaller and withdrawn.
- Limit ourselves by not taking risks personally or professionally.
- Prefer to stick with what we know, even if it's misery, rather than explore new opportunities and look for ways to grow.
- Accept situations rather than acting to make them better.
- Won't stand up for our needs or wants if it means rocking the boat.
- Think of ourselves as less important than other people—assume their needs and preferences must be more important than ours.
- Compensate for our unhappiness by shopping, eating, drinking, smoking—any activity that numbs us to our emptiness or pain.
- Develop any of a myriad of minor to grave physical manifestations of our internal upset including headaches, chronic fatigue, listlessness, and far more serious diseases.
- Prefer inactivity to action.
- Appear apathetic and passive.
- Opt to be followers.

When we are aligned with our core value of self-respect, we:

- Face reality even when it's difficult or painful.
- Take responsibility for our thoughts and actions.
- Are clear about our goals and dreams and map

out and prioritize actions to get us there.
- Believe we can accomplish whatever we set our minds to.
- Carry ourselves confidently and with purpose.
- Act with energy and optimism.
- Experience successes with the goals we set for ourselves.
- Take good care of ourselves.
- Claim our space and our role in our lives and in the world.
- Are assertive—but not aggressive. Calm and assertive is the most effective combination.
- Can and do take on the role of leadership.

Having self-respect versus not having self-respect is a difference in mind-set that has radical effects on our lives. When we are lacking, we become victims. When we are bursting with self-respect, nothing seems to stop us.

The key idea that we want to be clear on is that self-respect is a mindset. We can choose to believe in ourselves, to like ourselves, to consider ourselves worth standing up for and going the extra mile for. Or we can decide that we are not worth doing the work it takes to reach our goals and dreams. And guess what? Our life and our happiness will reflect what we have decided.

Why Self-Respect?
Self-respect is one of the indispensable values in our Five-to-Be-Alive formula. It's like the flour in a cookie. A cookie needs substance—flour is the foundational ingredient in a cookie, just as self-respect is in our lives. Without it, we would completely implode.

Put another way, when we have no self-respect or when

we are running low, it's like driving around life with our emergency brake on. It may not stop us from moving forward, but it is a constant drain on our energy and we don't get as far along in realizing our goals and dreams as we could.

Self-respect is a crucial energy for claiming our space in life. To distill the essence of self-respect to a simple illustration, we will use an example we see over and over again on the TV series "The Dog Whisperer." When dog owners complain of various behavioral issues with their pets, Dog Whisperer Cesar Millan comes to work with them. The unwanted dog behaviors are always corrected by changing the energy of the owners, not by training the dog to behave in certain ways. We want to emphasize this basic point: the key is changing the owner's energy by changing their attitude and outlook.

Dogs, like humans, are pack animals, and a dog and his/her person or people become a pack. In order for dogs to behave well in a pack, there can be only one leader and the rest are followers. When dogs misbehave, usually they feel that their owner(s) are not pack leaders. Their owners do not have self-respect and are not creating balance in the home, and therefore they do not have the respect of the pack. They do not claim their space or their role in the pack. And when the dog tries to fill the void and takes on the role of pack leader, his behavior can be in conflict with the owner.

Once owners decide to become calm and assertive leaders, the entire energy of the relationship with their dog shifts. And literally within minutes, in most cases, the dogs understand the energy shift in the pack dynamic and surrender to being followers to their humans. Once dogs know they can trust and respect their person, then their human has earned the position of balanced pack leader. But it takes constancy and consistency in order to stay pack leader. Self-respect requires us to always be aware of what energy we are embodying and to be able to shift it if we lapse into our old ways of lacking confidence. Literally, when dog owners stand up straight and square their shoulders (instead of slumping), look ahead (not down), and visualize positive outcomes with their dogs (instead of anticipating trouble), their dogs fall into line with their owners and their relationship becomes a partnership.

Liz and Zoe partnering on a walk.

The beauty in this example is that energy doesn't lie. We can tell ourselves all sorts of stories about whether or not we respect ourselves. But creatures who are tuned into our energy can read us, the authentic us, like a book.

When we want to change behavior we have to first decide that change is possible. The rest falls into place. When we truly embrace our role as pack leader in our lives, everything around us shifts. When we embody confident energy we have become the calm, balanced, assertive energy necessary to keep moving forward and to continue achieving our best possible life.

Love

The Basics
In a cookie, love is sugar. It is the sweetness in life, isn't it? But we're not talking about romantic love. When we discuss love as a value, we're talking about the bigger picture of love, meta-love—which includes caring, compassion, empathy, respect, trust, forgiveness, patience and selflessness.

Our love is a gift we more often think of sharing with others, but when training to live our best lives, love is a gift we need to share with ourselves as well. In fact, loving ourselves is what enables us to share love with others.

Compassion, forgiveness, patience, caring, respect and trust are ingredients we all need to use liberally towards ourselves as well as others in our journeys to our best lives. When we feel like we are stumbling along the way to our goals, or find ourselves up against challenges that seem as daunting as climbing Mt. Everest, frustration, anger and their ilk can seem like normal reactions, but they can be mightily destructive. As sugar is in our cookies, love is the sweetener that accentuates the positives in any situation and helps us find the best, most constructive ways to navigate through rough patches.

Alignment

When life is going smoothly, love feels easy. It's easier to see and appreciate the good in situations, in others, and in ourselves when we feel like we're on track and moving fluidly towards our best lives. Make sense? It's the same in relationships. When our sweetie-pies (be they spouses, significant others, children, family, or pets) are affectionate and loving it's easy to ooze love to them for all the wonderful support they share. When our sweetie-pies turn a bit sour on us, I think we can all relate that it can take a little extra *oomph* on our part to tap in to our preferred free-flowing level of love.

When we are working towards goals and building our best lives, we're going to run into a variety of disappointments, roadblocks, doubts, fears and commitment-sappers. All of which can make love seem to be an elusive commodity. But love is one of our ever-present and essential Five-to-Be-Alive values—it is always available to us and is always a critical component in growing into our life dreams.

You may already have tried-and-true strategies in nurturing love in tough times. We offer two simple but solid love solutions to add to your repertoire:

- We can only truly register one emotion in our brain at a time. So when we feel ourselves doubting our capabilities or feel like we want to give up on

ourselves, think of the reasons we love who we are and what kind of life we are creating. Once the love takes over in our head, there is no room for negative feelings. Focusing on love gives us a much-needed boost in positive, constructive directions. Remember, love is always present—we just have to choose to focus on it to bring it to the fore in any situation.
- When we are dealing with someone who seems to be incredibly difficult or negative, vigorously look for a quality or an understanding with this person you can connect with. The concept of *namaste* in yoga is to see and honor the light in someone else that is also in us. Practice seeing something good in people, particularly when they might seem vexing. It can be a mere iota, a glimmer of good. But once you connect with that, a much more positive relationship can grow.

Why Love?
Love is, as they say, what makes the world go 'round. We know love to be the uber-value that acts as a strong cup of cappuccino that warms us up and gets us going; a mega-vitamin that keeps us healthy and strong; and a fabulous dark chocolate treat that gives us that delicious tingly happy feeling inside when we are in our groove and being our most fabulous.

- Love heals.
- Love helps us soar when we might otherwise be tethered by doubt.
- Love helps us let go when it's time.
- Love gives us buoyancy— a resilience or optimism that translates to our life and our dreams.
- Love fuels our determination when weaker

commitments lose their staying power.
- Love is not just the end result, but integral to our process in all pursuits of passion.
- Love is our legacy. Of all our contributions in our life, love lasts.
- Love is a limitless resource.
- Love sometimes comes with foot rubs and flowers.

*Note: Please feel free to add to our love list. Its possibilities are endless.

Happiness

The Basics
How do you know happiness?

Often we equate smiling with feeling happiness. Yet, don't we sometimes force a smile when we'd rather scowl? Haven't we told people we are happy for them, when we were thinking quite the opposite?

Dogs offer another valuable illustration. Humans interpret tail wagging with dog happiness. However, there are tells in a tail wag that we don't read as instinctively as another dog would. A tail between the legs and sort of wagging is a sign of stress, not joy. A dog's erect tail might well be wagging mere seconds before they strike another.

So our outward indications of happiness aren't always reliable. They may mask something quite the opposite on the inside. It's that internal happiness—how we *experience* happiness—that we want to talk about nourishing.

Happiness includes a slew of gradations of this core

feeling. People describe happiness as a warm fuzzy, excited anticipation, positivity, optimism, pleasure, fulfillment, wild abandon, safety, fun. Designers measure happiness on a scale—if they are creating for consumers, they anticipate happiness to fall in this range:

- Comfort
- Contentment
- Joy
- Delight
- Bliss.

If we were making our values cookie, happiness would be the leavening—leavening comes from the Latin root meaning to enliven. The agent that buoys the cookie—gives it lift.

However we describe it or experience it, we likely all agree that happiness is a feeling we enjoy. Who wouldn't prefer to feel genuinely happy rather than sad? I'll take happy over angry any day. And we venture to say, happy trumps feeling afraid as well. Happiness is a feel-good experience.

We all desire happiness. It is one of our primal drives and motivating forces. So where does happiness come from?

We have been conditioned, if we are at all exposed to the media, that happiness is shiny, new, pretty, and pricey. Sexy sports cars, sultry glamour vixens, hotels where the elite go to play, even imported bottled water from glaciers…we may desire all these things, but, as we've talked about earlier, things do not bring us true happiness.

Happiness is not something we can purchase. Certain wonderful freedoms, choices and opportunities may come easier with money, but money cannot directly buy us happiness. Although advertising agencies have done an impressive job telling us otherwise, that $400 vacuum cleaner that is also a design icon in the Museum of Modern Art is not going to make us happy. It may give us a happy hit (and it had better make vacuuming effortless for that price-tag), but those benefits do not translate into genuine, long-term, life-sustaining happiness.

Two points we want to emphasize here. The happy hit we feel when we do have the good fortune to acquire something shiny, new, pretty and/or pricey is transitory. It doesn't last. It's much like having a sugar rush after having a huge bowl of ice cream for dinner. But then there's the inevitable crash. It's easy to become addicted to the happiness high—but it is temporary and always followed by a relative low.

Our second point is that happiness is indeed life-sustaining. Genuine, lasting, life-enduring happiness contributes to our good health. When we are depressed, our body chemistry differs from when we are happy. Studies indicate that people who report positive outlooks and being generally happy are healthier, and when they do get sick, they get well much faster than their depressed counterparts.

Laughter, an eruption of happiness, is even considered to be life-saving. Renowned journalist and author Norman Cousins credits his recovery from life-threatening heart disease to his commitment to laughter as the best medicine. He developed a recovery program that incorporated mega doses of vitamin C and belly laughs, induced by Marx Brothers films. As he reported, "I made the joyous discovery that ten minutes of genuine belly laughter had an anesthetic effect and would give me at least two hours of pain-free sleep." Indeed, medical studies show time and again that laughter reduces stress-related hormones and boosts our immune system.

We have a picture now of the kind of happiness we want to nurture. Not the quick artificial hit of manufactured happiness. Not pleasure, but the life-long sense of happiness and well-being that exists independently of our material or physical situation.

Martin Seligman, the father of Positive Psychology, proposed that a happy life is one that is:

- engaging,
- meaningful, and
- pleasurable.

Pleasure is not as important as feeling engaged in life and contributing in a meaningful way. Pleasure is more along the lines of getting that temporary happiness high. It's important, yes, but the engaging and meaningful aspects of happiness nurture consistently positive results when measuring happiness in our lives.

In aging populations in particular, research shows that those who choose to remain actively involved in life report higher levels of happiness than those who choose to be more withdrawn. People who feel fulfilled by what they do and find meaning in how they spend most of their energy—be it work, or raising a family, or pursuing hobbies, or volunteering—report the highest senses of well-being.

Alignment

How do we align with our happiness, and how do we create more happiness in our lives?

The recipe for aligning with our happiness is very simple. **First, identify what we love.** Ask yourself, what do I love to do? What pursuits of mine are in line with my interests and my values?

Even if we are not currently doing what we love, it's critically important to give our answer thoughtful consideration. We are talking about nothing less than creating lifelong happiness in our lives. Isn't that worth some thinking?

- Do I love working with people?
- Is a social component important to me?
- Do I want to work with children or elderly or underprivileged or physically challenged or artists?
- Are animals more my passion?
- Would farming or gardening bring me joy?
- Is technology what turns me on?

Once we land on the idea for how we want to focus our energy we are well on our way to being in alignment with our happiness.

Second, add meaning. What would add meaning for you in the pursuit of your choice? If you want to bake and sell the world's best cookies, please send us some! We're kidding. We are serious, however, about creating your cookie enterprise in a way that will reward you with fulfillment on a meaningful level.

Meaning often comes when we create a challenge for ourselves—setting realistic goals and challenges are key in building in a sense of purpose and achievement to our process. We also feel a sense of meaning from our endeavor when we derive an emotional reward from it. Perhaps you could mentor students or underprivileged youth or retired people. Perhaps you could support your community by sourcing all your ingredients from local and organic farms. Perhaps your cookie sales can bring awareness to and support a cause that is dear to you. What is going to elevate this pursuit from being just your commitment to being your passion?

Our third step in the happiness recipe? **Do more of what you love**. Engaged, meaningful, and pleasurable—more, more, more.

To recap, the basic recipe for life-sustaining happiness is:

- Identify what you love.
- Add meaning.
- Do more of what you love.

While we are creating and aligning ourselves with our happiness, an important facet to remember in the recipe is balance. Doing more of what we love does create an enduring sense of well-being and happiness in our lives. But we are happiest when we are in balance. So we benefit most when we consciously divvy up our focus and energy between work, play, and love.

If we are all work and no play, we are out of balance. If we are rich with love and play, but engage in no work, we will be out of balance. Our lives will be lopsided, just like the cookie we build without a key ingredient. If these three aspects overlap in our lives, where work is also play and love is all around, then we have a fabulous blend! However work, love and play shake out in our lives, they each need our nurturing and they each need our happiness.

And speaking of nurturing, community and sharing are important to happiness. Individuals can certainly experience high levels of happiness, but communities provide much-needed support, particularly in tough times. It also feeds our happiness to share it. When we do what we love and are able to share that with others, not only do we benefit from the much-needed social interaction (we are not islands, after all), but sharing our strengths and our joy enhances our sense of purpose and meaning. Not to mention the recipients of our sharing probably appreciate it as well.

So, when designing our best and happiest lives, remember to balance these three pursuits:

- Work,
- Play, and
- Love.

And remember to share our happiness with others.

Measures of happiness are fairly subjective and open to interpretation. We each know best if we are happy and to what degree. Personally, I know that I am happy every morning to wake up, swing my feet onto the floor, and step into my day with a healthy mind and body. And I will continue to make life choices that allow me to feel that happiness every morning and share it throughout each day.

Why Happiness?

As a value, happiness nurtures a multitude of positives in our lives. Topping most people's short lists for what they want from life, happiness is a non-negotiable. Everyone wants to be happy. And for more good reasons than you might think.

Happiness:

- Leads to overall better life-long physical, mental and emotional health.
- Creates lower blood pressure, stronger hearts and stronger arteries.
- Contributes to faster recovery from illness and surgery.
- Lengthens our life-expectancy.
- Decreases experiences of depression.
- Increases support from friends and the richness of our social interactions.
- Keeps us young.
- Gives us more energy.
- Generates optimism and creative solutions to challenges in our path.
- Fuels us in moving toward our dreams.
- Is infectious and can positively impact the people around us.
- Is enjoyable, fun, a gift.

Gratitude

The Basics

Gratitude is a value that accentuates our happiness factor. When we exercise our awareness of gratitude, we experience a more profound happiness that carries us through no matter what challenges we may face.

Our experience of gratitude is typically a feeling of thankfulness and appreciation. When someone helps us out—whether they open the door for us when our hands are full, or whether they help take care of us when we're sick—we feel grateful for their time, caring, and attention. It's relatively easy to experience gratitude around things others do for us.

But gratitude is so much more than being appreciative for what others do. Reasons to be grateful are everywhere. Aren't we also grateful for things like good health, for love, for family, for doing fulfilling work, even for having a good night's sleep? The more we are aware of all that we appreciate, the more powerful a player gratitude will become in our lives.

Alignment
Like any other value or skill we want to develop, we must practice gratitude. To bring ourselves into alignment with how we value gratitude, we offer three easy exercises we can practice daily.

Make a Gratitude Board
Have you heard of or created for yourself a vision board? Vision boards are a collection of images and words you may find in magazines and such that you collage onto a poster board that remind you what you aspire to. A gratitude board is a collage of images and key words from your current life that remind you of reasons you are grateful. They could be family photos, images of your hobbies and passions, representations of good health, community groups that are important to you, ways you contribute that are meaningful to you…all the reasons you are currently thankful on a daily basis. If we create such a collage and place it in a spot we can see it every

Amy (top) and Liz (bottom) both create Gratitude Boards

day—on our refrigerator, our bedroom door, our bathroom mirror—we heighten our consciousness of how rich our life is. The more we are aware of all the reasons we are grateful, the bigger the benefit we experience from this value.

Daily Gratitude Journal
In a dedicated notebook, at the end of every day jot down five things that happened to you that day for which you were grateful. They can be minute or hugely impactful. The idea in this exercise is to become a daily practitioner of gratitude. And after a few weeks of keeping a gratitude journal, we suspect you will notice a shift in your overall sense of optimism and positivity, which permeates the rest of your interactions and experiences.

1. **Say thank you and mean it.** We often say thank you out of habit, without really thinking about it. Two things are important in this exercise: verbally acknowledging gratitude and saying it with consciousness. Thank you really soars for everyone involved when we feel it as we speak it.

Why Gratitude?
In our nutritious and delicious values cookie, gratitude is the butter. It greases the wheels for all the ingredients to come together and work fabulously as a whole.

Gratitude, while being a foundational value and a key contributor to our happiness, generates tangible benefits that help us in achieving our goals. Gratitude also sets for us a mental tenor that raises our appreciation and awareness of all the gifts in our lives as we move through our challenges. We gain an overriding sense of optimism when we embrace gratitude as one of our Five-to-Be-Alive values.

Gratitude is a value that has long been espoused in the spiritual and religious realms, but not so much in the scientific realm until recently. Lately, scientists have found significant connections between the practice of gratitude (our three exercises above are easy ways to practice) and well-being benefits.

The regular practice of gratitude:

- Makes us more likely to achieve personal goals.
- Elevates our physical activity and exercise levels, which reduces stress and its physical toll.
- Enhances our energy, attentiveness, enthusiasm, determination, vitality, alertness and overall well-being.
- Boosts our optimism and general positive attitude.
- Gives us a greater sense of connection to others.
- Increases our empathy and our likelihood of being supportive, sharing with and helping others.
- Decreases the importance we place on material possessions and increases the value we experience in our relationships.

Five-to-Be-Alive in the Real World

Now that we have our *mise en place* set— we have all Five-to-Be-Alive ingredients at our fingertips—we are almost ready to look at practical ways to fine-tune our daily actions with our values so that we can get on with designing and living the lives of our dreams. But before we discuss how to best implement our values on a daily basis, we need to briefly revisit the outside influences on our values systems.

Outside Influences

We all have a pretty impressive internal fortitude, whether it feels that way or not. If we decided that we were truly ready to make changes in our lives, we could become wholly accountable to our commitments. But none of us lives in a vacuum. The people and social structures we live with and interact with shape our behaviors and, at a deeper level, our values. It's important, for this reason, to take a look at those influences to see where our values are being reinforced and where they might be weakened.

If we surround ourselves with people and institutions that share our value systems, but particularly our Five-to-Be-Alive values, then those very values will be nourished and reinforced by our environment. On the other hand, if we live among people and institutions that do not share our values, we would plausibly and subconsciously feel pressure to behave against our own values and in alignment with those of the larger community.

FAMILY

Taking a look around at our immediate influences—those may be significant others, family, close friends—the people with whom

Values is a conscious way of life and conversation topic in the Bailey household.

we share our lives most frequently and at the most familiar level are also our role models. Parents, of course, are models for children. Extended family and close friends also shape our behaviors. One of the most primal ways we learn is by example, and when we see people we trust and respect consistently modeling certain characteristics, we tend to mirror those. And if we behave a certain way for a long enough time, we eventually adopt those behaviors and values as our own.

How would you rate your family and inner circle on reinforcing the value of accountability? Self-respect? Love? Happiness? Gratitude?

SCHOOL
Schools are another primary source where young minds are profoundly shaped. Some of our school systems are struggling merely to educate. Modeling constructive values may not be something they can give much thought and time to. All schools have rules of conduct, but the values behind that conduct are not necessarily explored or consistently modeled for the children.

If you have children, do you get the sense that their school builds accountability awareness and practice? Self-respect awareness and practice? Love awareness and practice? Happiness awareness and practice? Gratitude awareness and practice?

COMMUNITY
Our immediate communities include our neighborhood, our culture, our apartment complex or subdivision. Our neighbors, our book clubs, homeowner associations, neighborhood watch associations, volunteer organizations, all the groups close to home that we

belong to shape our values.

Do these groups place a premium on accountability? Self-respect? Love? Happiness? Gratitude?

RELIGION
Religious institutions, to the extent that we may be involved in any, are prime sources for teaching values. Values seem to be rooted in the very bedrock of religious teachings and practice. And hopefully, our religious institutions also model the values they espouse. But this is not necessarily always the case. As with all of our external influences, they merit examination to determine if they truly embody the values that are important to us.

Do you observe, in your practice of religion, that it supports the value of accountability? Self-respect? Love? Happiness? Gratitude?

WORK
If we are employed and/or work at home, we likely spend a significant amount of our time at work or on the job. Written or unwritten, workplaces usually have codes of practice, protocol, ethics, mission statements, codes of conduct—all manner of guidelines for behavior, performance expectations, and professional goals with respect to individual employees and the company at large. Even if we are self-employed, we probably have our own set of professional guidelines covering conduct, ethics and mission statement.

- *Do you work with people and organizations that value accountability—100%, mostly, somewhat, when it's convenient, rarely? How does that line up with your need for accountability?*

- *Do you work with people and organizations that value self-respect—100%, mostly, somewhat, when it's convenient, rarely? How does that line up with your need for self-respect?*
- *Do you work with people and organizations that value love—100%, mostly, somewhat, when it's convenient, rarely? How does that line up with your need for love?*
- *Do you work with people and organizations that value happiness—100%, mostly, somewhat, when it's convenient, rarely? How does that line up with your need for happiness?*
- *Do you work with people and organizations that value gratitude—100%, mostly, somewhat, when it's convenient, rarely? How does that line up with your need for gratitude?*

How does your values support system rate?

After examining how your outside influences support your practice of the Five-to-Be-Alive values, do you find that accountability, self-respect, happiness, love, and gratitude are reinforced or brushed off?

Do you need to make shifts in your colleagues, your work, your religion, your friends, your community, your clubs so that you are better supported in practicing the Five-to-Be-Alive?

Just being aware of how well you are supported (or not) in your values practices, is critical in keeping on track with the Five-to-Be-Alive and the life-changing benefits they can bring.

Chapter 4

Seeing Our Values

We believe living in alignment with our values, and in particular our Five-to-Be-Alive values, is the key to unlocking our best life. Consciously making choices that line our actions up with our values will successfully navigate us through whatever challenges come our way.

Before we can successfully maximize the benefits of living in tune with our personal values, however, we must first be able to see them.

- In theory, what are the values you live by? What values do you think you embody?
- In actuality, how in line with those values are you? What values do your actions reflect?

The answers to these questions could surprise us. We may find that, to varying degrees, we think one way, and act another.

When we are not in the habit of seeing our actions as manifestations of the values they represent, it's like watching a 3D movie without the 3D glasses. The images are fuzzy. But once we put on the lenses we can see vividly the action around us. Think of the exercises in this chapter as essentially putting on your values spectacles. Our values become crystal clear once we look at life through that lens. And it then becomes much easier to sort out how to live in alignment with them.

Looking at life without awareness of our values creates an unfocused, unclear experience.

When we realize that our actions are manifestations of our values, we experience clarity in our life.

Values are everywhere. They are behind every choice we make in our day. Every action from the moment we wake to the moment we go to sleep is motivated by our values. We may not think of our behaviors this way, but if we looked at any random day in our lives, we could plot where our actions stray from our values. That is an essential discovery—where do we ignore the values that are important to us? Think of this discovery process as creating a treasure map to unlocking the powers we already possess to living our best possible life.

To help us get started on our quest to pinpoint our personal values, we created a Value Map.

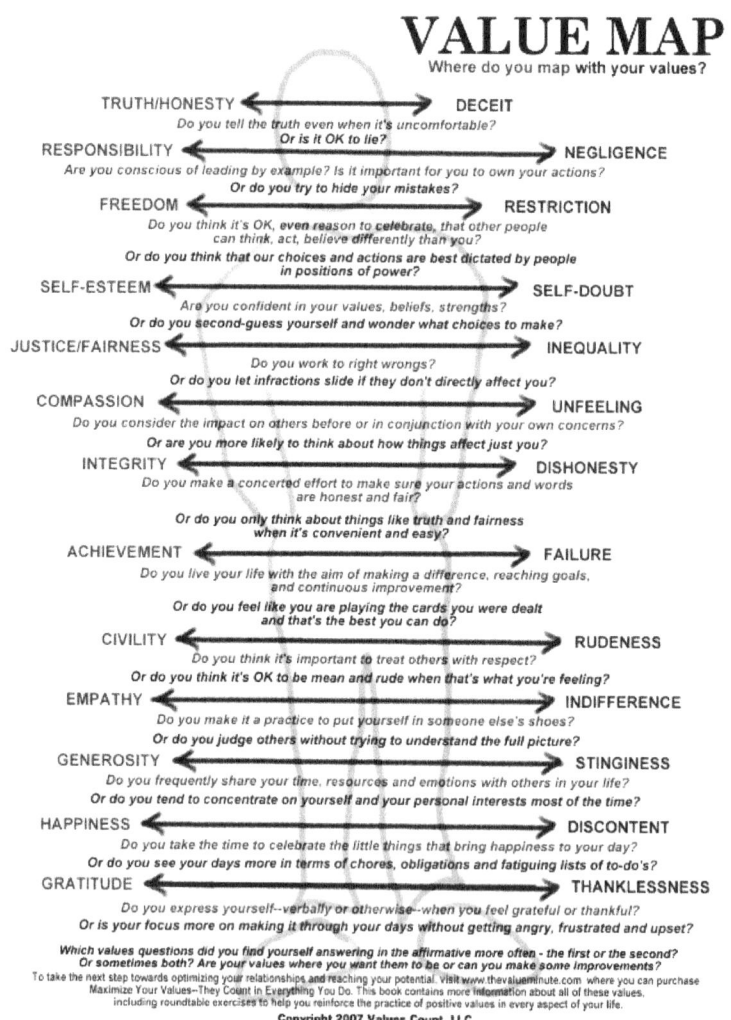

As you can see from our Value Map, we have illustrated thirteen common values as a sliding scale range. The questions below each value help us see where we land on the scale between the values at each end. The first question under each arrow pertains to the value on the left side of the scale; the second question pertains to the value on the right end of the scale.

This is the first step in our discovery process—where do we exist on the scale? For example, I might think I'm an empathetic person, but maybe I tend more towards indifference than I realized. However we answer, this is not an exercise in judgment. We simply want to have a clear picture of which values are our current primary guides. Which values do we act upon consistently?

Please read through the questions on the Value Map and plot on the scale where you think you stand in relation to the two opposing values. This map will help you get a broad feel for who you are in terms of your values. Our next step will be a detailed exploration of the power in our life-changing Five-to-Be-Alive values.

Seeing Our Values: Personal Values Assessment

Our Five-to-Be-Alive values—**accountability, self-respect, happiness, love, and gratitude**—are the core values that can literally transform our current lives into the life of our dreams. So let's explore these five values to discover how important we think they are and see to what degree we practice each of them in our daily life.

Generally, we don't go through our days hyper-conscious of our values, measuring how we line up with our values with each choice we make. Our values, whatever they are, are ingrained in us so that we are not always conscious of their impact on our daily decision-making. This is great if we are in tune with our core values and acting in alignment with them. But when we want to make changes in our lives or in how we behave, it is particularly important to take our values pulse, so to speak—to see and be mindful of what values we reinforce.

For each of the Five-to-Be-Alive values, we offer a list of Personal Values Assessment statements. As you read each, rate your reaction without taking much time to think. Our initial responses are often our truest, before we have a chance to reflect and edit to make them seem "more acceptable". On a scale of 1-10, 10 being you wholeheartedly agree and think or behave that way all (or most all) of the time, and 1 being you never (or almost never) think or behave that way, give a numerical ranking to each statement. Again, rate each as quickly and honestly as possible.

Once we go through the measurements for each value, our score will give us a sense of whether each of the Five-to-Be-Alive values is one that we practice well already, or whether we see opportunities to practice each value more consciously in our day-to-day.

Accountability Assessment:

1. I consciously lead by example.

2. I behave in ways my mom would be proud of; that my children would be proud of.

3. It is important to me to take responsibility for or to own up to my actions.

4. I behave in ways that make me feel I've done my best.

5. If I had the chance to live my day over, I would be at peace with my choices.

6. If I could live my day over again, I would not change most of my behaviors most days.

7. My actions do not cause me to lose sleep at night.

8. I am rarely embarrassed by the choices I make or how I behave.

9. When things don't go as I planned, I look for new solutions.

10. When things don't go as I planned, I stay calm and don't give up.

11. I don't try to hide my mistakes.

12. I do not look to blame others when decisions I made have negative outcomes.
    TOTAL:

13. *I feel accountability is a value that I need to practice more in day-to-day life.*

Total Score 1-12

1-35   You are not an accountable person.
36-60   You are rarely an accountable person.
61-84   You are sometimes an accountable person.
85-108   You are frequently an accountable person.
109-120   You are almost always an accountable person.

How does your answer for #13 match up with your assessment?

Self-Respect Assessment:

1. I am confident in my beliefs and in knowing what is important to me.

2. I am confident in who I am and what my strengths are.

3. I feel that I consistently make decisions on what is best for me and what is in line with my values.

4. I walk assuredly, with head held high and shoulders back.

5. I feel good about standing by my decisions throughout my life.

6. I rarely second-guess myself and wonder what choices to make.

7. I rarely seek the counsel of friends and colleagues before making most decisions.

8. I rarely feel confused and unclear about making choices in my life.

9. I do not attempt to hide or shrink from attention.

10. I do not constantly apologize to people.
    TOTAL:

11. *I feel self-respect is a value that I need to practice more in day-to-day life.*

Total Score 1-10
1-30	You have a very unhealthy level of self-respect.
31-60	You often have an unhealthy level of self-respect.
61-83	You sometimes have a healthy level of self-respect.
84-100	You have a healthy level of self-respect most or all of the time.

How does your answer for #11 match up with your assessment?

Happiness Assessment:

1. I celebrate the little things that bring happiness to my day.
2. I laugh every day.
3. I smile every day.
4. I feel that my life has meaning.
5. I am excited about the possibilities my day holds when I wake each morning.
6. I see my life as a big adventure.
7. I am fulfilled.
8. I feel optimistic, even when the chips are down.
9. I do not feel that my life is empty and meaningless.
10. I do not see my days as lists of to-do's, obligations and chores.
11. I am not sad or tired most of the time.
12. I do not rely on food or drink or other boosts to make me happy.
13. I am not looking for ways to escape my life.
14. I am not constantly seeking something to look forward to.
    TOTAL:
15. *I feel happiness is a value that I need more of in day-to-day life.*

Total Score 1-14

1-40	You are unhappy most of the time.
41-70	You are unhappy frequently.
71-90	You are sometimes happy.
91-110	You are frequently happy.
111-140	You are happy most or all of time.

How does your answer for #15 match up with your assessment?

Love Assessment:

1. I love me.
2. I approach new people with a positive attitude.
3. I enjoy spending time with me.
4. I have things that I love to do.
5. In other people, I look for things that I love about them.
6. I feel that I am worthy of being loved.
7. I am happy when taking good care of myself and others.
8. I do not tend to see other people as different and potentially threatening.
9. I am rarely often angry with or jealous of others.
10. I rarely prefer that people keep their distance.
11. I prefer to share good things with people I care about.
    TOTAL:
12. *I feel love is a value that I need to practice more in day-to-day life.*

Total Score 1-11

1-33	You rarely feel love or share it with others.
34-60	You sometimes feel love and share it with others.
61-84	You often feel love and share it with others.
85-110	You feel and share love most or all of the time.

How does your answer for #12 match up with your assessment?

Gratitude Assessment:

1. I express my gratitude, verbally or otherwise, when I feel thankful.
2. I *feel* it when I say "thank you" to people.
3. Even when I am having a challenging day, I focus on the good things in my life.
4. In tough situations, I still find reasons to be thankful.
5. When my day seems to go downhill, I refuse to be blinded by everything that is going wrong.
6. I would describe my outlook, in general, as a glass half-full.
7. When I say "thank you" it is not a robotic, knee-jerk reaction.
8. My focus is not just on making it through each day without getting angry, frustrated, or upset.

TOTAL:

9. *I feel gratitude is a value that I need to practice more in day-to-day life.*

Total Score 1-8

1-24   You are not a grateful person.
25-48   You infrequently feel grateful and/or express gratitude.
49-64   You sometimes feel grateful and/or express gratitude.
1-80   You feel grateful and/or express gratitude most or all of the time.

How does your answer for #9 match up with your assessment?

In looking over your assessment scores for each of the Five-to-Be-Alive values, do you see opportunities in your day to heighten the practice of each value?

Do you practice accountability consistently? Where might you be more accountable? What will you do to be more consciously accountable every day?

Do you practice self-respect consistently? Where might you need more self-respect? What will you do to consciously practice more self-respect every day?

Do you practice happiness consistently? Where might you find more happiness in your interactions? What will you do to consciously experience more happiness every day?

Do you practice love consistently? Where might you practice more love? What will you do to be consciously practice more love every day?

Do you practice gratitude consistently? Where might you practice more gratitude? What will you do to be more consciously grateful every day?

Values as Daily Tools: Seeing Benefits

As we've seen, our Five-to-Be-Alive values help us work through and rise above any and all challenges and goals. You name it, our values play into every decision and action we make. When we consciously act with our values as our guide, getting through the day becomes a much easier and more successful process.

We've taken a handful of comments we hear over and over—plans and dreams we can probably all identify with—to quickly run through how a simple values dose works in helping us achieve any kind of hurdle, mini or mega. We've used broad strokes here in illustrating how values play into mapping out the steps that take us toward our goals. This will help you use values to your advantage when we start to create Personal Values Plans in the next chapter.

I want to feed myself and my family healthily, but we are on a tight budget.
Buying organic, buying lots of produce and whole foods is great but not always easy when pinching pennies. Here's how values practice plays in.

Accountability—you decide this is a priority and you take the steps to feed your family smartly:

- Grow some herbs and produce in your yard or in pots at your home.
- Join a community garden where you share costs and harvest.
- Stretch your dollar by cooking with high-nutrient but cheaper foods like cabbage, protein-enriched pasta, quinoa, etc.

- Buy frozen instead of fresh produce—it's usually cheaper and lasts longer.
- Buy in bulk.
- Eat less meat. Beans and rice together make a perfect protein.

I want to exercise regularly but don't have the time.
Adding an exercise component to an existing commitment in your day is easier than you think. Multitask.

Self-Respect—exercise and being fit are important to you and how well you feel. Involve others so you get social time out of it as well.

- Walk or bicycle as many places as possible in your daily routine.
- Walk or jog with your dog and your family—to have quality time together while exercising.
- Instead of coffee breaks, spend that time doing yoga stretches or plyometrics for an instant recharge.
- Get up 30 minutes early (or more) and devote that time to exercise.
- Instead of social time with friends at a bar or restaurant, socialize while working out together.
- Exercise while watching TV.
- Take the stairs whenever possible. If you are in good health, sprint up stairs for short cardio bursts.

My family doesn't spend any time together—we're all too busy.
With everyone's busy work and social calendars, it can feel like you are all ships passing in the night. But families need each other, and we all need a break from our hectic

schedules.

Love and Happiness—families can get a recharge from being together that will refresh them and enable them to go back to routines happier and energized.

Accountability plays in here as well, as everyone needs to commit to spending regular time together.

- Agree on spending at least one family meal together during the week. Aim for as many as possible, but starting with one is a good way to build that custom. No TV, no radio, no phones, texting or Internet. Just share and catch up with everyone. You could even make a game out of it—everyone reports on another family member: what they've been doing, what made them happy that week, what made them sad, what they are working on, who is inspiring them, etc.
- Pick a time on the weekend where everyone spends an hour or two doing chores around the house and then as a reward, you all have a treat together—like pancakes or smoothies or pizza.
- Take a family retreat every month or couple of months—where you all spend a weekend together playing, creating something, catching up.
- Set aside regular times each week to exercise together.
- Cook together,
- Volunteer together.
- Walk the dog together.

My love life has gone stale.
People who have been in relationships for a while sometimes feel they are in a rut. Their love lives may feel

predictable and boring. They miss the "spark" and want it back.

Love, Happiness and Gratitude are key players here. Shake it up together as if you are partners in exploring all kinds of new experiences. And consciously practice thanks for your other half. That always helps the love.

- Start date night (if you're in a relationship) where every week or two you alternate planning a date together.
- Try something new together—it can be a seemingly unrelated activity, like rock climbing—just something new for both of you to experience together.
- Do little things differently—just to change things up from the regular routine.
- Write each other love notes.
- Tell each other every day one reason you are grateful for the other.

I'd like to lose a couple pounds.
Many people, at some point in their lives, have felt the desire or need to shed a few pounds. The whole idea can feel like a drag—whether it's five pounds or fifty—as most view losing weight as an undesirable chore.

Accountability and Self-Respect—the recipe here is generally to burn more calories than you consume. There are countless ways to go about shedding pounds, but whatever your path, you commit to taking specific steps with the end goal of feeling better and being healthier.

- Commit in writing to your goal.
- Post your goal in places you will always see it.

- Stock your kitchen with foods that will help you healthily slim down.
- Commit to exercising more or more effectively.
- Ask someone to be your coach in the process so you regularly must be accountable to them.

I wish I felt younger.
We all want to feel our best and be as healthy and energetic as we can for our age. When faced with the physical changes that come with aging, it's important to feel good, no matter what your driver's license says.

Happiness and Self-Respect—feeling healthy and being healthy adds profoundly to our happiness and our sense of self-confidence. Keep these goals in mind when designing your plan.

- Commit to getting more sleep.
- Eat healthier foods.
- Stretch and exercise daily.
- Drink lots of water.
- Laugh more.
- Look for joy in every situation and interaction.
- Start thinking, "Yes I can!"
- Try something new you've resisted attempting because you felt you were "too old."
- Let go and enjoy where the adventure takes you.

I'm exhausted all the time—I want to feel less tired.
Our lives are extremely busy. Most of us are on the go from the moment we wake up, so it's understandable when we feel tired. But if we're tired all the time, if we constantly feel spent and unmotivated, something may be out of kilter in our life that may have nothing to do with how much sleep we are getting.

Accountability—if becoming energized is a priority for you, committing to the steps that will get you there is a key value in this process (once you've ruled out any medical issue that might cause your exhaustion).

- Prioritize time to sleep if you are short on sleep time.
- Regularly exercise to recharge your system.
- Drink less caffeine and eat less sugar.
- Drink more water.
- Make sure you get enough protein in your diet.
- Picture yourself consistently as a vital, energetic, positive person.
- List the steps you are taking to get recharged and check them off daily so you are reminded of where you can improve.

<u>*I want to find work that I enjoy and pays the bills.*</u>
Many look at work as a necessary evil, but it can be incredibly positive and enriching.

Happiness and Self-Respect—are two key values that will keep you on task and motivated to find fulfilling work. **Gratitude** is also a key player in creating enjoyment in the work you do find.

- Identify your strengths and what skill sets you love to use.
- What activity or pursuit is truly your passion?
- Be specific about what kind of work you really want.
- Articulate to yourself what you want.
- Spread the word and network with people about your commitment to the kind of work you envision.
- Market yourself in creative ways.

- List 3 reasons each day how the work you do reminds you to feel thankful.

Do you see how values are the backbone to successfully meeting our goals? Once we see how our values directly guide our actions and outcomes, and once we have a clear map of our personal values system, then we are ready to create our path to our best possible life.

We are ready for our values alignment. Much like a good sports therapist tweaks our muscular-skeletal systems into alignment, we are going to bring our actions and choices into alignment with our Five-to-Be-Alive values. And once we are in flow with our core five values, we are well on our way to successfully living our dreams!

Chapter 5

Personal Values Plans—Blueprint for Aligning with our Five-to-Be-Alive Values

Once we start seeing through our values lens and are able to true-up our everyday actions to match our personal values, we can start to reap the benefits of living in alignment with our values. To powerfully put our values to work for us, we have created a series of quick steps that will plot our course to achieve any goal we set for ourselves.

For each goal or dream we want to make reality, it is crucial to create a Personal Values Plan (PVP). Our plan aligns our values practices so we can use the power of the Five-to-Be-Alive to achieve our goals. Whether we aspire to lofty, life-altering dreams, or whether we want to refine our processes or lives on a smaller scale, our Personal Values Plan is the blueprint that provides us with the essential steps for success.

We will step through a sample PVP so you can see how it works and how it creates a tailor-made plan for you to follow where you will see success in each of your goals, no matter how small or grand. Each plan can take just a few minutes to complete, but when followed, the plans can create a lifetime of positive change.

We will examine the whys behind each step, the power in the process, and the payoffs in the end. Ultimately, these

PVPs are your blueprints to living your best possible life.

While we have included both a sample plan and a blank plan for you to personalize, all the worksheets you need for assembling your Personal Values Plan are available upon request by emailing us at info@thevaluesgals.com or via our website, www.thevaluesgals.com, on the Contact Us page. That way, you can print them and fill them out so you have a clear checklist for getting to each goal and beyond.

Each PVP is just a few straightforward steps to complete. We will list them for you first, then fill in the sample PVP so you have a detailed example on each step of the process.

Ready to see it in action? Ready to get in alignment with your best life? Let's go!

Personal Values Plan: Overview
1. Declare your goal.
2. State your level of commitment to this goal and any qualifications affecting this goal.
3. List the practical steps to reaching this goal.
4. Choose the top 3 of the Five-to-Be-Alive values that, when practiced, will most help in achieving this goal.
5. Create action steps to live in alignment with each of your top 3 values for this goal.
6. Identify the top 5 anticipated benefits of the process to achieve this goal.
7. List up to 5 of your desired payoffs from reaching the goal.
8. Commit to the Personal Values Plan.
9. Post-Achievement Review (optional)

Personal Values Plan: Sample
1. Declare your goal.
   > *I will broaden my profession and income sources to include documentary photography.* **(note that my language choice here is intentional—not "I will try to" or "I want to," but "I will." It's a stronger choice and carries with it more power when stating our goals. So when choosing your language, don't weaken your intentions with wimpy words!)*

2. State your level of commitment to this goal and any qualifications affecting this goal.
   > Is there a timeframe for completion?

   > *Yes. By summer of 2009, I want to be earn-*

ing money each month with photography. Even if it's just one session a month.

What kind of priority is this goal? Rank it on a scale of 1-10, 1 being the lowest priority, 10 being the top priority. Include any explanation that will help you gain clarity on this priority.

Photography is a number 2 priority. My first professional priority is to continue to get producing projects and earn the majority of my income that way. Building photography as a profession and income stream is priority number 2.

Is it conditional on achieving other goals first? If so, please list each here and complete Personal Values Plans on any prerequisite goal(s).

No. I already own the equipment I need, know my strengths, and shoot every week to continue fine-tuning my eye. I have my portfolio on my website now and my photography business cards. I am visualizing photography as a profession and am speaking about it whenever I can.

3. List the practical steps to reaching this goal. In the order you plan to start each step, what are the logical and necessary actions you will take to reach your goal? (Please add more steps as needed.)
    a.   *Shoot maybe 5 more friends in*

hour-long documentary photo sessions so I can practice shooting and delivering for a "client"

b.   Ask for testimonials from the friends and "clients" I shot for free.

c.   Offer a specially-priced hour-long documentary photo session to friends and colleagues for professional or personal portraits to continue getting comfortable shooting clients, to gain marketing opportunities by referral.

d.   Create a PDF marketing piece to email to potential clients offering moderately-priced hour-long documentary sessions for people in their professional environment or for people in docu portraits with their family, friends, and/or pets.

e.   Email marketing materials to potential clients consistently, pegging the marketing materials and timing to special event opportunities as well.

f.   Continue to submit photos for publication in NatGeo, JPG and other online contests—to gain credibility and notice.

g.   Look for opportunities to hang an image in a gallery show— to gain credibility and notice.

4.   Choose the top 3 of the Five-to-Be-Alive values

that, when practiced, will most help in achieving this goal.

> Which three of the Five-to-Be Alive values—**love, gratitude, accountability, self-respect, and happiness**—are the most powerful tools in getting you to your goal? And why?
>
> a. ***Happiness***—*photography immediately puts a smile on my face. The process brings me great joy and I love seeing some of the images that I am able to capture. I particularly adore capturing moments (important and seemingly mundane) and sharing those images with people who appreciate them for their meaning, memory, or visual beauty. The more I can shoot and share the results, the happier I am. It's a creative process that completely absorbs, challenges and rewards me. And this happiness spreads into all other areas of my life, making it a win-win.*
>
> b. ***Self-Respect***—*to live the life I want to live (which is to be a freelancer of creative pursuits who is not tied to living in a particular location), I will take the steps I need to take to birth my photography passion into a profession,*
>
> c. ***Gratitude***—*I am so grateful to have found something I enjoy immensely and that brings joy as well as meaning (I am conscious of bringing a reporter's eye to telling truths through images or exposing*

situations or relationships that are thought-provoking) that I want to share that ability and that energy with the world. I am a better person when I am creatively fulfilled, challenged and in the flow, which in turn allows me to be a better contributor to the relationships and responsibilities in my life. Being conscious about staying in tune with the energy of gratitude will also, I think, translate in positive ways to the people who hire me to shoot.

5. Create action steps to live in alignment with each of your top 3 values for this goal. (Please add more steps as needed.)

   If Love:
       a.
       b.
       c.
       d.
       e.

   If Gratitude:
       a. *Every evening, list at least 2 reasons in my gratitude journal why I'm thankful for all that photography brings to my life.*
       b. *Every morning, before I start the day, focus for one minute on how grateful I am to be doing what I love to do.*
       c. *In my communications with any clients or potential clients, always include an expression of sincere thanks.*
       d.

e.

If Accountability:
   a.
   b.
   c.
   d.
   e.

If Self-Respect:
   a. *I will ask clients for testimonials and/or referrals to help me market my services.*
   b. *I will be clear in setting expectations for clients so that they are clear what strengths and styles I bring to the table and we can be on the same page in collaborating on creating what they want.*
   c. *I will not give my services away (unless for a charitable cause or as a gift). My time and talents are worth my fee.*
   d.
   e.

If Happiness:
   a. *Shoot photos each week that are just for fun or are for me... that make me happy.*
   b. *Bring an energy of joy to each shoot.*
   c. *Explore something new every week... a new subject, a new style, a new approach... keep the process fresh.*
   d.
   e.

6. Identify the top 5 anticipated benefits of the process to achieve this goal.

a. Becoming a stronger shooter.
   b. *Becoming more proficient technically.*
   c. *Becoming more comfortable in getting images clients love, in the allotted time.*
   a. *Knowing light and my camera settings better.*
   b. *Being a better, faster creative problem-solver.*
   f. *Generating a happy and loyal client/fan base.*

7. List up to 5 of your desired payoffs from reaching the goal.

   a. *Being able to move away from my current city for extended periods of time*
   b. *Being able to earn a living from photography, no matter where I live.*
   c. *Growing as a photographer and fine-tuning my eye and photographic skills.*
   d. *Contributing to photography in terms of developing my niche of documentary-style portraits of people.*
   e. *Through photography, helping people see (the world, relationships, situations, themselves) in new ways.*

8. Commit to the Personal Values Plan.
   Declare your commitment to this goal by signing this oath to yourself:

   I ____Liz Stubbs___, on the _20th_ day of _March_, _2009_, do promise myself that I will diligently, consistently, and energetically follow the above steps that I created in my Personal Values Plan to achieve this particular goal:

I will broaden my profession and income sources to include documentary photography.

9. Post-Achievement Review (optional). Once you have achieved your goal, go back through your plan and compare how the actual process stacked up against your Personal Values Plan worksheet.
    - Did you honor your commitment to the plan and follow the plan consistently?
    - Did you modify your goal once you had started working your Personal Values Plan?
    - Did you do another Personal Values Plan worksheet if you did modify your goal partway through the process?
    - Were the benefits and payoffs as you imagined or were there some bonus benefits in the process?

Personal Values Plan: Template for Personal Goals

1. Declare your goal.
    Clearly and specifically, state your goal.

2. State your level of commitment to this goal and any qualifications affecting this goal.
    Is there a timeframe for completion?

    What kind of priority is this goal? Rank it on a scale of 1-10, 1 being the lowest priority, 10 being the top priority. Include any explanation that will help you gain clarity on this priority.

    Is it conditional on achieving other goals first? If so, please list each here and complete Personal Values Plans on any prerequisite goal(s).

3. List the practical steps to reaching this goal. In the order you plan to start each step, what are the logical and necessary actions you will take to reach your goal? (Please add more steps as needed.)

    a.

b.

   c.

   d.

   e.

   f.

   g.

4. Choose the top 3 of the Five-to-Be-Alive values that, when practiced, will most help in achieving this goal.
   Which three of the Five-to-Be-Alive values—**love, gratitude, accountability, self-respect, and happiness**—are the most powerful tools in getting you to your goal? And why?

   a.

   b.

   c.

5. Create action steps to live in alignment with each of your top 3 values for this goal. (Please add more steps as needed.)

   If Love:
       a.
       b.

       c.
       d.
       e.

If Gratitude:
       a.
       b.
       c.
       d.
       e.

If Accountability:
       a.
       b.
       c.
       d.
       e.

If Self-Respect:
       a.
       b.
       c.
       d.
       e.

If Happiness:
       a.
       b.
       c.
       d.
       e.

6. Identify the top 5 anticipated benefits of the process to achieve this goal.

a.
   b.
   c.
   d.
   e.

7. List up to 5 of your desired payoffs from reaching the goal.

   a.
   b.
   c.
   d.
   e..

8. Commit to the Personal Values Plan. Declare your commitment to this goal by signing this oath to yourself:

   I _____, on the _____ day of _____, _____, do promise myself that I will diligently, consistently, and energetically follow the above steps that I created in my Personal Values Plan to achieve this particular goal:

   Your Signature

9. Post-Achievement Review (optional). Once you have achieved your goal, go back through your plan and compare how the actual process stacked up against your Personal Values Plan worksheet.

- Did you honor your commitment to the plan and follow the plan consistently?
- Did you modify your goal once you had started working your Personal Values Plan?
- Did you do another Personal Values Plan worksheet if you did modify your goal partway through the process?
- Were the benefits and payoffs as you imagined or were there some bonus benefits in the process?

Chapter 6

The Five in Practice: Reaching Your Goals

In this chapter we have identified nine areas that we repeatedly see as areas of interest for people looking to make improvements in their lives. These are all timely topics that we think are also timeless. These are not meant to be substitutes for your own Personal Values Plan (PVP) as they are not PVPs themselves, but you may find them to be useful in supplementing your plans. You may also find that some of what we've written in this chapter actually fits right into your PVP, and if that's the case, by all means recycle it (we're into recycling!).

The purpose here is to show you how you can take a big, beneficial, life-altering goal, apply our Five-to-Be-Alive values to it to get the results you want or need. The areas we address here with our Five-to-Be-Alive approach are:

- **Better Health,**
- **Green Living,**
- **Improved Financial Station,**
- **Realizing Our Dreams,**
- **Better Relationships,**
- **Career/Work Improvements,**
- **Finding/Preserving Love,**
- **Simplifying Your Life and**
- **Weight Loss.**

Keep in mind as you read through each of the following sections that the information we provide is meant to be thought-provoking, it is meant to show how the Five-to-

Be-Alive values play into reaching your goals. We offer our thoughts, suggestions and guidance representing our vision as to how the Five-to-Be-Alive and other values can impact your plans. It is important for you—the one who knows you best—to take what you can use from these pages then add to it and customize it to best meet your particular situation.

We have interspersed many of our own personal stories in this chapter. We, too, have wanted and needed to make changes or improvements in our own lives in some of the nine areas we discuss here. We hope our personal stories will help energize you further to reach your goals.

Your Five-to-Be-Alive for Better Health

1. Self-Respect

Good health is something we can be proud of when we look in the mirror and see ourselves standing tall, with color in our cheeks and light in our eyes, looking fit and well. But also, and perhaps more importantly, good health makes us **feel** good from the inside-out… living pain-free, being capable of physically performing all we ask of ourselves throughout the day, maintaining good levels of physical fitness, feeling light and energized and, well, healthy. If we are in good health but feel as if we can be in better health, attention to how strong and capable and free we will feel and be when we achieve this goal will keep us tuned in to our self-respect. Better health creates a better us. And we want the best for ourselves, yes? Keep focusing on the personal payoffs of good health. There are infinite ways we can improve our health but choosing and practicing balance in our lives will go a long way to our goal.

- **Achieve balance in your life.** All work and no play does not lead to good health. Neither does the reverse. Work, play, passions, relationships, exercise, nutrition, community... a balance of these makes for happy and healthy people.
- **Practice Zen.** Find time in each day to have chill-out time or me-time. Whether that's meditation or walking or exercising or yoga or some activity where we are disconnected from the chaos and cacophony of our busy stressful lives and can have some moments of peace and calm. Our body and mind need this time to recharge and refuel to keep all its systems in optimal working condition.

2. Happiness

Happiness is a fundamental need for all of us. And indeed, it creates good mental and physical states. Physiologically, laughter has positive effects on us, even when we're ill. But some of the most deeply-rooted paths to happiness are to build connections with people and to be in the practice of seeing the good even if it's easier to see the bad.

- **Laugh often.** Real belly shakers. Listen to comedy routines, watch funny movies, get together and laugh with friends and family. Take advantage of witty banter opportunities to add a little levity to your day. There's a lot of funny in everyday stuff—Jerry Seinfeld was a master at pointing out comedy in the mundane. Laughter is physically and mentally fabulous for us.
- **Connect with your community**—whether that's geographic, professional, religious, athletic, family, friends, hobbyists. Strong community support and

connections are a characteristic of people who live long and happily.
- **Practice a positive outlook.** When you choose to see the world as full of possibilities rather than obstacles—the glass half-full rather than half-empty—such a positive and hopeful outlook translates into benefits physiologically as well as mentally. Our body is a finely-tuned instrument that often follows our lead when we give it direction. If we believe that we can do something, very often we can. We certainly can't do something if we believe we will fail. Want to be in better health? Believe that you will be.

3. Accountability

Better health is a measurable goal. Whatever better means to you, there are measurements and indicators to let you know when you've gotten there. Whether that means you drop 5 pounds, shrink 2 inches, run 10 seconds faster per mile, walk up 4 flights without being winded, drop those cholesterol numbers…set those specific goals and keep working towards them until you achieve them. Accountability will keep us on task. So set little steps along the way and pat yourself on your well-deserving back as you progress toward your ultimate goal!

- **Exercise daily**—create a regular workout plan that matches your current fitness level. Gradually increase time and/or intensity to elevate your fitness level. Balance strength training with aerobic exercise. Even gardening and cleaning provide good exercise. Set modest goals for improvement and continue to raise the bar or plan to maintain once you reach your ultimate goal.

- **Home, not hospitals.** Have as your goal to not be a patient in a hospital. Keep good health as a top priority. Commitments to preventive health care, good nutrition, daily exercise, mental wellness can keep us healthy, happy and away from being regulars at our doctor's office.

4. Gratitude

One of the quickest ways to keep on track towards a goal or to keep positive when the going gets tough is to focus on gratitude. I may not be in the best shape or the best health, but I am grateful to be able to do X, perform Y, feel well and content most of the time. When the doubts or fears or routine of life threatens to affect your better health plan, it's helpful to actively practice gratitude. Give back... even if it's just time on the phone with a friend who needs to talk. Give of yourself and gratitude will follow.

- **Contribute in a way that is meaningful to you**. People who find meaning in their lives feel fulfilled in positive ways. Volunteer, mentor, be an advocate for a cause you believe in, teach or tutor, share your time, knowledge or compassion. In the process, you will also be someone for whom others are grateful.

5. Love

Love plays a key role in good health. Love for our mates, our children, our friends, our profession, our pets, ourselves, the world we live in—love keeps us inspired and motivated to be the best we can be for us and for others.

- **Practice love.** Do what you love for a living, and if that does not yet seem possible, choose to find joy, even if just an iota, in your current professional situation. Practice love also with the people with whom you spend time. Sometimes we can all get on each other's nerves, no matter how dear we are to each other. In those moments especially, focus on why you love the people you are with. Even if joy seems elusive at times and it feels difficult to find the love, we can usually find the positive lessons/growth opportunities in situations, if we look.

Other Values That Will Help You Reach Your Better Health Goal

1. Honesty
We may be tempted to cut corners and opt for what feels like the easy or cheaper way out, choosing pre-packaged, non-organic foods. And while some pre-packaged are far better than others and certain foods are more important to choose organic vs. non-organic, always keep your eye on the big picture—your health and well-being. Telling ourselves that cutting corners here and there is a slippery slope. It can revert back to a standard way of being and our commitment to better health can go out the window.

2. Growth
Even things that we know are good for us like exercise and better eating can feel like daunting tasks and we can wonder whether we can ever reach our goals. Better health is the best possible gift we can give ourselves and our loved ones. When we are healthy, everything is

better. We function better, we feel better, and our bank accounts aren't plagued by hefty bills that can rack up when we are seriously ill. Look at this goal as a gift of personal growth. No matter how challenged you feel some days, keep your eye on the prize and celebrate how much you are growing in personal strength and commitment in the process.

3. Serenity

When we are healthy, we feel good. And when we physically feel good, that translates into a mental and emotional serenity as well. And who doesn't like and benefit from a little more serenity in our lives?

A Few Practical Steps Towards Better Health

- Basic simple practices like washing our hands, staying hydrated, and getting good quality and enough sleep can go a long way in keeping us healthy.
- Good nutrition—we are what we eat. Our body needs regular intake of vitamins, minerals, proteins, good fats, good carbs, fiber and plenty of water to keep us energized and healthy. Processed food, bad fats, loads of sweeteners, and chemical-laden foods or even an imbalance of foods can wreak havoc on our bodies and lead to medical complications and expenses.
- Do not smoke cigarettes.
- Drink alcohol moderately.

Helpful Resources

Seek health information from a variety of sources and schools of thought and do what makes sense to you—

whether you are sick and looking for a treatment plan, or whether you are healthy and want to stay that way. Look to your conventional medical model, alternative options, Eastern medicine, nutritional, spiritual—read what others have tried and had success with. Ask questions. Get second opinions Don't hesitate to challenge what doesn't make sense to you or for you. Understand what institution or agenda may be backing a medical solution or plan. Drug companies, for example, are a for-profit business with the intent to make money and sell drugs, not necessarily to make us healthy without drugs.

Personal Story: Optimizing and Maintaining My Best Health

Good health is something I don't take for granted anymore. When I was a child, I was blissfully healthy except for the occasional flu and cold and that bout with the chicken pox. But I never thought about health being something I needed to protect or safeguard.

However, once in my 30s and now having turned 40 (and the clock keeps ticking), a shocking number of people in my circles of family, friends and colleagues have come down with serious illnesses and some have lost their battles. It's quite a cautionary tale.

I have always been robustly healthy and I have always led a fairly healthy lifestyle—I think the two are directly related. I am active, exercise daily, don't smoke, drink probably just a couple bottles of wine in a year, take nutritional supplements, and my diet is Kosher and pescetarian, largely without white flour and sugar, and organic… but I realized in the past several years that

I could step up the health focus. And with the health struggles I have witnessed my friends and family going through, it is of the utmost importance to me to stay healthy and to stay out of the hospital. I don't even like to take aspirin—you can imagine how averse I would be to IV bags and daily dosages of anything medicinal... other than dark chocolate.

It can be overwhelming to try to figure out the best strategies to get healthy and stay healthy. It seems that there are contradictory reports and studies on every aspect... from whether or not coffee is good for you to whether daily vitamins make a difference. It does require some research so you can see what information makes the most sense for you and your health goals and lifestyle. And it requires diligence—sticking with your health and wellness plan once you construct it. But the Five-to-Be-Alive values have steered me to determine the best comprehensive health plan for me and enabled me to stick with it.

*First, there's **happiness**. I think we can all agree that healthiness is happiness. When my body is too ill or ill-prepared to do what I ask it to, I'm not a happy camper. I'm a runner. About every other year I run a marathon and the years in between I run shorter distances. I love to snowboard and play with my dog and work on the farm with my boyfriend, and my producing gigs often require long days on my feet. If I wasn't physically up for any or all of those things I love to do, I would be terribly sad. When I FEEL healthy and physically well-tuned, that is the foundation of my happiness. And if I were to ever face a serious illness, I would feel scared at not being able to count on my typical good health.*

*Happiness plays into **gratitude**. Every run I take, every morning I get out of bed feeling spry, every walk I venture on with my dog where I get to enjoy watching her romp and play... I am grateful for being healthy. And the gratitude actually washes over me sometimes like tingles up and down my spine. Health is wealth. I have so many options available to me because I am physically able, because I am strong, limber, and my mind is still nimble. I can't imagine anything more important than my health and I am grateful daily that it's doing well.*

Love plays into my health plan right along with the fish oil. I love my family and those dear to me and I want to be here with them and for them. Taking good care of my health is actually an expression of love for those in my life. I want to share our experiences, our ups and downs, and I want to be able to be supportive when they need me. How am I to do that if I don't take care of myself? The balance to that is that I want to participate fully in my own life as well and to pursue my dreams and contribute to this world in ways that are meaningful to me. I simply can't do any of that without good health. Love and health, I think, feed off each other. It's well documented that overwhelming stress can cause and aggravate illness. Love, on the flip side, can work miracles.

Love motivates Liz to take optimal care of herself.

Self-respect is a pretty fundamental value when it comes to living healthily. I may want to eat those hockey-puck sized gooey, iced, warm cinnamon confections every time I smell them when waiting for my plane in the airport. But instead, I think about my arteries and heart pumping my blood effortlessly without all that buildup obstructing the flow. I think about my digestive system searching through the aftermath of such an indulgence seeking something to feed my brain and my muscles so that I can continue through my day without a sugar crash and food coma. I want to give my body the best foods it needs so that I can look and feel young, be healthy, and have the fuel I need to get through my ambitious schedule. There's a lot I want to be doing in life. And respecting the needs of my body is the basis of achieving my goals.

My dog counts on me for daily walks and love and care and a roof over her head. My boyfriend counts on my love and spirit. My clients count on my generating creative projects on time and on budget. My friends and family count on me for support, laughs, whatever they feel I bring to the relationship. **Accountability**—it's ever-present. People (and a pup) depend on me. And I depend on me. Health is a priority for me and I am the guardian of that commitment.

While I have a lot of specifics I could share about what I do to be healthy, that isn't the aim of our conversation here. What enables me to stay on track with the constant vigilance around my best possible health are a pragmatic sense of balance, choosing to live in a positive manner, and the five most critical values in the toolbox, the Five-to-Be-Alive values. —Liz

Your Five-to-Be-Alive for Green Living

1. Self-Respect

So you want to live green? Well then, you shall. If you decide green living or at least greener living is important to you, then self-respect is a value that will help you achieve this goal. You want to be healthy and live in a healthy environment, right? So choose green steps that directly affect your health… whether that means increasing your exercise over your consumption of fossil fuels or whether that means living as chemical-free as you can—green can help you build a healthier life and lifestyle.

- **Streamline transportation**—be efficient about getting from point A to point B and all parts in between. Carpool, use public transport, bicycle, drive your car only when you can accomplish 3+ errands and map your route for the most efficient fuel usage, drive a hybrid.
- **Go natural**. Choose natural foods, cleaners, clothes—pay attention to using consumables that have low environmental impacts in their production, transport, and disposal.
- **Reduce chemicals**—in cleaners, on plants, in building materials and home furnishings. Instead of using detergent, bug spray, glass cleaners, dry-cleaning services, carpeting, etc. that you've always used… read the labels and go for chemical-free options.

2. Happiness

Digging our fingers in the dirt can be an incredible joy. Re-connecting with nature and the seasons and cycles of growth and creation can bring us a whole new level of enjoyment. Syncing with nature's rhythms and cycles can reset a lot of our natural rhythms that we lose when we are disconnected from nature. For example, let's examine how we can reconnect with nature and live greener with something we all need and consume daily—our food. When we are conscious about eating foods as they are in season, we naturally build in a welcome variety of nutrients into our menus throughout the year. Also, when we grow the food we eat, not only are we saving money but the food is often much tastier and healthier.

- **Grow our own food.** Loads of us are now growing vegetable gardens in our front yards and in pots on our patios and fire escapes. We don't have to live on a farm to experience the joy of planting and nurturing and dining on herbs, fruits and veggies that we grew ourselves.

3. Accountability

If you want to live greener, hold yourself and your suppliers to the same standards. Not only must you take green steps that you can measure, like recycling, but spend your dollars on products and with companies who share your green values and practices.

- **Re-use, repurpose, recycle**—repair clothes, appliances, furniture that can be salvaged; repurpose items into other uses; wash and re-use plastic bags and aluminum foil; recycle plastic, metal, junk mail, paper, glass, batteries; turn food scraps into compost for your garden.
- **Purchase recycled materials**—paper, packaging, building materials, clothing, etc.

- **Green suppliers.** Research the companies you buy from and don't support companies that clearcut trees, aren't committed to green values, who poison our waterways with chemicals, pump feed animals with drugs or force feed them foodlot feeds that they wouldn't normally eat in nature, farm with GMO seeds, or who don't practice recycling themselves.

4. **Gratitude**

When we live in the city or densely populated suburbs and feel disconnected from nature, we can forget what a treasure being in nature is and how delicate a balance we live in with nature. In the urban jungle, we don't often see or think about the coal that was mined in dangerous conditions to provide our power, or the sewage that we create that has to be cleaned and dispersed, or the mountains of trash that we create every day that have to be safely disposed of, or even where the food comes from that magically appears on our grocery store shelves. How often are we grateful for these basic items—power, food, clean water, or a clean city? One of the most impactful ways for us to practice gratitude for our basic utilities is to be as efficient as possible about their use.

- **Live off the grid**—use solar power, catch rain water, create a/c with air flow in your building design, and insulate for heat
- **Reduce use.** If living off the grid isn't a choice you are able or ready to make, simply reduce your use of utilities. Use energy-saving appliances, unplug and turn off when you are not using them, use collected rain water or water from your shower

for your plants, insulate your home better. Even if it feels like you are taking tiny steps and making refinements rather than sweeping changes, that's a positive step. Every little bit makes a big difference in the global picture.

5. Love

Green love extends from you to your family, your pets and your planet. With love as a key value, you want to nurture cycle-of-life patterns that do not cause harm to people, animals or to the environment.

- **No suffering.** Don't use products (cosmetics, shampoos and soaps, cleaners, drugs) tested on animals.
- **Leave no footprint.** With energy and resources, be as efficient as possible, and minimize waste—treat them as if they are precious, because they are.
- **Group green.** Think green for your pet products as well. Your pet family deserves to live chemical-free and to contribute positively to a green lifestyle as well.

Other Values That Will Help You Reach Your Green Living Goal

1. Ecological Responsibility

When we feel a responsibility to be good to our earth and when we want to live a less wasteful life, green living is a perfect fit for our lifestyles. Our planet is the only one we have and when we understand how many species we have caused to become extinct, when we realize how much of the world doesn't have access to clean water, when we see how much fuel we consume in our cars and homes, we can discover countless new ways to become more energy-efficient, to live cleaner and live with far less impact on other species and environs, and we can become more actively involved in global ecological education and awareness-raising.

2. Creativity

There's nothing our creativity loves more than a challenge. Sure there are easy ways to power our appliances—conventional electricity, gas, batteries. But wouldn't it be fun and cheaper to power our appliances off the grid? Hollywood actor Ed Begley, Jr. rides his stationary bicycle to power what he needs to make breakfast in the morning. Alternative power sources are readily available even to those of us living in prime power company territory. Want to live differently? Want to live green? Scratch that creative itch!

3. Stability

Prefer not to be surprised every month with escalating food and energy costs? Go green. Plant your own food gardens, explore alternative energy sources, use alternative energy vehicles. Cut the conventional energy and food umbilical cord wherever you can and choose green.

A Few Practical Steps Towards Green Living

- Fabric shopping bags aren't just for groceries. Use them for your retail purchases as well.
- Buy products with minimal packaging.
- Turn off and unplug—don't use appliances and electrical equipment when they aren't necessary, and when they aren't in use, turn them off and unplug them.

Helpful Resources

1. Internet
- www.green.msn.com
- www.thegreenguide.com
- www.treehugger.com

2. Community groups

3. Classes at local home supply stores

4. Green-living do-it-yourself TV shows

Personal Story: Getting to a Greener Existence

"Going green" is quite the movement these days. Protecting the environment has always been important but it took until this most recent decade for it to be viewed as "cool" or "trendy" or "popular". Some credit Al Gore and his documentary "An Inconvenient Truth" for singeing the dire, truly frightening reality onto our brains, others point to the spiking gas prices we endured for years or

crazy weather patterns for getting people to pay attention. I'm not really sure what spurred our family into becoming more aware of our carbon footprints but over the past five years we've been trying to make a concerted effort to change the way in which we live and move about in our world with the goal of having a net-positive impact on our environment—or at least a less negative one.

One of the bigger steps we took was buying a Hybrid vehicle. In 2006 my husband's vehicle was in need of a replacement. At the time gas prices were soaring and we were becoming more and more educated about the impact of pollution on our environment. Both of these factors contributed to our seeking a Hybrid vehicle. To be honest, I think the better gas mileage makes my husband the happiest but reducing our negative impact on the environment does bring him satisfaction. Either way, it's all good.

I think the biggest hurdle for me in terms of "going green" was coming to the realization that just because it was this huge thing didn't mean I couldn't effect change. That taking baby steps and doing little things could indeed make a difference; that I or my family may be one tiny little piece to the solution but when you put all of the individuals and families like us together—all of us doing those little things—it becomes a big thing and makes a big impact. So, changing one light bulb might seem ridiculous but what if a million people changed one light bulb? I had to start thinking that way. I had to stop thinking of myself and my family as a tiny blip; that our minor efforts didn't matter. I also had to realize and accept that we had financial constraints and that we may not be able to do everything we could as a result. Some of those bigger ticket items would have to be put on my

G^3 list—Going Green Goals. So no, we aren't doing all that we can do but we are doing something and doing something is better than doing nothing. I've had to remind myself of that when I feel like we're not doing enough or when I'm frustrated by not being able to do more.

Here are things my family and I have/are doing (and will continue to do) and have changed or have become more mindful of in order to reach the goal of living a greener life:

- *Purchased energy-efficient light bulbs to replace incandescent bulbs as they burn out.*
- *Purchased a Hybrid vehicle.*
- *Replaced our gas-powered lawn mower with a battery-powered mower.*
- *Replaced our gas-powered weedeater with a battery-powered model.*
- *Replaced our gas-powered blower with a battery-powered model.*
- *Replaced our inefficient dial thermostat with a digital thermostat.*
- *Stopped using the heat cycle on our dishwasher to dry the dishes.*
- *Cut back on water consumption by doing things like turning water off as we brushed our teeth and limiting shower durations.*
- *Recycling as much as we can.*
- *Depending on natural light as much as we can and turning off lights when they are not needed.*
- *Purchased cloth/environmentally friendly bags to use when shopping.*
- *Purchasing locally grown produce/products when available/possible.*
- *Supporting/contributing to causes that*

are committed to improving/sustaining the environment.

These are just some examples. There is more we want to do. We want to make our home more energy efficient— new windows and more energy efficient appliances would make a difference. That's a longer-term goal. There are other things, however, on my list that are easier to accomplish. Things like walking to more places to run

Walking is a green way to locomote -- and great exercise too!

errands when possible; composting; collecting rain water for reuse. If you think about it, there are little things we can all be doing that cost nothing and that take nothing but a little time and maybe a little planning.

So why are we doing these things? Because going green is important to me. I am **grateful** *for this world we live in. I appreciate nature and all that it has to offer. I appreciate and* **love** *life. I want my children, grandchildren and beyond to be able to enjoy a quality life here on this*

*Earth. I feel it is my **responsibility** to do what I can to help make that happen. I fear that humans, like polar bears and other animals are today, will be a threatened species in the not too distant future. It makes me **happy** to do whatever I can to make a difference. I feel good about making whatever contribution I can make. My family and I are making a difference and that makes me happy. —Amy*

Your Five-to-Be-Alive for Improved Financial Station

1. Self-Respect
Everyone can identify with the self-respect value that we want to be able to enjoy the financial freedom to make key choices about our lives and how we live. We want to be able to choose where we live—specifically, in a safe neighborhood, in a comfortable home, close to certain locations, amenities, services or people. We want to have the financial comfort to take care of not just our needs—food, shelter, health—but our joys and dreams as well. Particularly when our national and world economies are suffering, we all are acutely aware of wanting to shore up our own financial health and improve our financial station. Having financial freedom is closely tied to our value of self-respect. There are many steps we can take along this path, but our basic first step is to spend less than we earn.

- **Live within our means**—do not use credit cards for purchases we can't pay off at the end of the billing cycle, do not use store credit cards, pay in cash, do not accept 0% interest deals that simply postpone payments.

2. Happiness
Imagine feeling happy that you've saved money rather than spent money! You have options when you have money in hand and in your treasure chest, not obligations. When you are facing bills you feel stressed about paying, do you feel happy? NO! So build in happy hits to your money strategies…

every time you find a way to save rather than spend deserves a mini-celebration. (NOT a spending celebration☺ ... but think about taking a time-out for you to enjoy something you love to do... walk in the park, read a novel, hold your squeeze's hand... mini-celebrations come in unending fabulous and free options!)

- **Value saving**—list all the perks of saving rather than spending and focus on the relaxation and positive feelings that come from keeping money rather than frittering it away.

3. Accountability

Make a specific financial plan on paper or on your computer as to how you will save money and/or improve your financial station. Once you commit a plan to paper, your value of accountability can kick in. You will see very easily where you stay on your plan, where you stray from the plan, where the plan can be improved to enhance your financial situation even more.

- **Spend less**—cut expenses, spend only on necessities (mortgage, utilities, groceries), shop for best rates and deals, trim what you think you can trim and then challenge yourself to cut 20% more [forego manicures, pedicures and hair coloring, get your hair cut less frequently, brown bag your lunch, don't eat out except on special occasions, brew your own morning coffee, cut premium cable channels, work out at home and cancel your gym membership, wash your own car instead of getting it detailed, instead of girls' night out have the girls over for potluck and dish,

instead of movie theater prices, rent, use coupons online and in stores, make your payments on-time to avoid late fees
- **Attack plan.** Make paying off credit card and high-interest debt a priority—before you take a vacation, pay down debt. Before you get a newer car, pay down debt. Pay more towards your highest-interest loans so they get paid off first.

4. Gratitude

When we bring our focus to gratitude that tends to re-energize us. Even if our current financial station is not where we desire it to be, practice being consciously grateful every day about the positives in our monetary situation. Track your progress and be grateful for the small dents you make. When we focus on the positives, we bring more of them into our lives and we consciously head in the right direction.

5. Love

Love the feeling you have when you are really gaining ground on a goal? Love the feeling you have when you are taking good care of you and of the ones you love? Practice love when you are on track for improving your financial situation.

- **Energize your earnings**—earn efficiently: seek higher-paying opportunities, are there passive income options you can pursue that will make money for you while you are earning money on the job? Have items around your house you never use? Sell them!

Other Values That Will Help You Reach Your Improved Financial Station Goal

1. Inner Harmony
If you want to live without unnecessary stress and worry (and who wouldn't benefit from lightening those loads?), focus on the inner harmony you feel as you spend less, save more, and shed your debt. Inner harmony is priceless and debt demons can completely sabotage that state of mind and way of being. When it gets challenging, mentally go to your place of inner harmony and remind yourself that this is your end result.

2. Pleasure
When we improve our financial station, we have more choices. We can choose to buy organic foods, or to see a doctor about non-emergency health improvements, or to take a class we've always wanted to take, or to take a vacation. Pleasure is a state of mind and being that we all enjoy and it has health benefits. When we are able to enjoy pleasures, our body relaxes and is not plagued by the physical degradations that come when we are constantly stressed over money.

3. Helping Others
If helping others is a value that is important to us, improving our financial station can afford us the ability to practice that value. Whether we prefer to donate to causes or charity or whether we prefer to be actively involved in volunteering, an improved financial station can make that desire a reality.

A Few Practical Steps Towards Improving Your Financial Station

We can all probably find ways to save more, stretch our dollars a little farther, and spend less. Cut little expenses across the board and enjoy the larger savings—they all add up to a better bottom line: cut premium cable channels, make coffee instead of purchasing at the café, search for the cheapest gas when filling up, use coupons, color your own hair, stock up when your necessities go on sale, make meals instead of eating out.

Helpful Resources

1. Internet
The Internet. as always, can offer a wealth of *free* information and advice. For example, you can get advice on how to create a budget. Many good ideas for cutting back or saving can be found on the Internet.

2. Financial News/Publications
Several news channels offer regular financial news reports where useful resources are cited. Consider purchasing or checking out a book or publication from a library that you feel will help you reach the financial goals that you have.

2. Financial Advisor
Many financial advisors offer their services for free. While you should always be cautious with your money, there are trustworthy individuals and businesses that can assist you with your financial needs. Just remember to get references and do your homework before hiring anyone or turning any financial records over to anyone.

3. Support Groups/Friends

Having someone to talk to about your struggles can help you stick to your plan. Don't hesitate to join a support group or ask a close friend to help you "just say no" on those shopping trips!

Personal Story: Earning Hard-Won Financial Freedom

One of the most overwhelming challenges that I have faced is the substantial credit card debt that I allowed myself to take on in a relationship and business partnership in my early 20s. He and I were living together and starting a video production business together. And somehow it evolved that I would work as a manager at a home theater/movie rental store while he launched our business. On top of using my earnings to live on, I allowed close to $40,000 in startup costs and living expenses for the both of us to rack up on my credit cards.

You can read the writing on the wall, right? Our relationship was strained on several levels. And when I discovered proof that he was starting a relationship with another woman, I moved out immediately. But I had no legal recourse to force him to pay his share of the debt, all of which was in my name. Even though he promised to do his part, after we eventually found our way to speaking constructively, I never saw a dime.

I made lots of rookie mistakes in this scenario. We had dreams of being together and making successful films. But dreams don't become reality without doing the work it takes. And that just didn't happen. I like to think of it as earning a Ph.D. in life. It probably cost close to the same tuition.

But in terms of getting back on my feet again, it took a while. I was exceptionally fortunate that friends came to my rescue and invited me to live with them until I could rent a place on my own. I don't know what I would have done without them. I lived many states away from any family. These friends were literally guardian angels.

My professional life started to take shape, and slowly I joined up with a production company and learned the ropes and began earning a bit better than retail wages. It wasn't enough to make a dent in my debt, but it became enough to allow me to pay rent on my own and keep afloat on all the other expenses.

For many years, however, I was consumed by shame. Prior to this debt albatross, I had always been one to pay for everything as soon as the bill came due. I didn't carry credit card balances. I had no debt. And now I was buried in it. And for what I considered to be foolish, unwise reasons. I was embarrassed that I was in my 20s and saddled with such serious debt. And with nothing to show for it—It wasn't a mortgage or a car, after all.

I was also drowning in resentment. Because I was the one making the minimum payments every month, I was unable to put money aside for things that I wanted to do, like travel. My choices were limited. I felt shackled—I had extremely limited options in life because my first responsibility was to make these infernal minimum payments. I resented being the only one ponying up for the debt both of us created. It was all-consuming.

I was never one for whom budgets and financial plans made a lot of sense. Normally, my practice would have been to spend less than I earn. And that had always worked out for me. Numbers make my head swim. And I was too ashamed to seek help from any kind of financial advisor—I didn't know how I would afford one anyway. Since 1995, I have been a freelancer—I have not had a salary or a regular project or paycheck. Income was not predictable and sometimes felt like a roller coaster with periods of feast and famine. I didn't know how I was ever going to get out of debt, and it's fair to say I was in despair.

Enter my tide-turning, life-changing values.

I was fast tired of the bleak picture I painted for myself. Once I made the decision to rid myself of the past's chokehold and pain, everything shifted. **Accountability** *turned the tide for me. I had wasted so much energy blaming my ex-boyfriend for being a shmuck, and abandoning his responsibility for paying off the debt and leaving me with the credit card bills that I wasn't acknowledging my responsibility in the outcome. It was excruciatingly uncomfortable, but the fact is I allowed myself to get into this horrific (to me) debt situation. And it was going to be me that got me out of it. So I consciously decided that I would stop wishing reality were different, and I took on paying down the credit cards.*

Once I took ownership of paying off the debt, I stopped writing in my journal about how upset I was about my ex abdicating his responsibility. I stopped articulating that I wished he would pay up. I even wrote his mother a letter, as I was no longer in touch with him, to tell her that I wished them both well. All energy I formerly channeled to resentment and disgust and shame, I now diverted to making money, I became devoted to rebuilding my financial strength. I hardly ever said "no" to a gig. I took projects that I may not have had the experience for, but I worked with fabulous teams and learned as I went. I always paid more than the minimum on my balances due. And when I got chunks of money, it gave me great pleasure to pay off and close out cards and loans. I was accountable to no one but myself, and I wanted to rebuild a me who was financially free to make the best choices in life.

***Self-respect**—boy, did I want that back. Once I stopped beating myself up and being ashamed for being so in debt and stopped thinking of myself as foolish and unable to get my head above water, I saw myself as someone who was living with integrity. I was doing the right thing. And there's nothing to be ashamed of when you are making good on your commitments. I was able to talk about my debt without hanging my head. It was important, also, for me to climb this mountain. I had a generous offer to bail me out, but I thought it was critically important for me to close the loop and pay off my past myself. I'm not above being rescued, and am grateful for the offer, but I didn't want anyone else to pay for debt they hadn't incurred.*

***Love**. I'm worth it. It took me a while to really own that. I used to feel other people were more valuable or worthy of sacrifice than me. But I know now that loving myself is not selfish. I have to take care of myself if I am to have anything to give to others and to the world. And I am committed to making choices that are good for me.*

Living in the present (not the past), and taking control over what had overwhelmed and scared me was the best gift I could give myself. Once I shed the debt-related shame and fear, I found a freedom and balance that I hadn't had before. And all my relationships, especially my relationship with me, blossomed. I was lovable to myself again. And I think when I have a good relationship with myself that that translates directly to all my relationships.

*Needless to say, I was a much **happier** person for empowering myself and being on the path to financial freedom. Every time I made a big payment or paid off an account completely, I was elated. And with each debt I paid, I was able to put the money that would have gone to debt, towards experiences that brought me happiness—like travel. To me, experience is wealth. Mostly, I was happy identifying myself as a person who was doing what was right and moving forward towards an increasingly more positive and liberated life.*

*And last, but certainly not least, is **gratitude**. I am unspeakably grateful that I have been fortunate enough to have the kind of work and to have been busy professionally, earning so that I have been able to make that mountain of debt merely a memory. And I am eternally grateful to everyone along the way who supported me with compassion, respect, and encouragement at every step on my road back to solvency.*

These five core values were my blueprint to conquering one of the most seemingly overwhelming challenges I had yet faced. Financial plans, the desire to be out of debt, working hard... those were not enough to make my goal a reality. It took this essential combination of Five-to-Be-Alive values to transform my desire to be debt-free into an accomplishment. —Liz

Your Five-to-Be-Alive for Realizing Our Dreams

1. Self-Respect

Your work or your profession may involve your contributing to your employer's dreams. Your parenting efforts may involve facilitating your children's dreams. Your volunteer efforts may be helping an organization reach a defined goal. Hopefully, your dreams overlap with the people's dreams to which you contribute. Perhaps part of realizing your dreams is helping other people's dreams come to fruition. But in order for us to feel whole, fulfilled, and to truly realize our respect for ourselves, we must build towards our own dreams as well. It's a balance. We can give towards others' dreams, and that's fantastic, but in order for us to continue to be able to give to others, we must also give to ourselves. Make a plan, with steps included, to move towards realizing your dreams. What are they and what will it take to get there?

- **Listen** to and **trust** your inner guide.
- **Stay true** to what you believe.
- **Organize** your living and work space—clear your clutter—clutter saps us from focus, serenity, efficiency.
- **Take big risks**—practice by taking little risks, or stretches every day—if you follow your instincts, they will lead you in the direction that's best for you.
- **Think big** but keep a healthy perspective. Becoming an astronaut may not be feasible depending on your physical capabilities and medical health, but working for NASA may be.

2. Happiness

Realizing our dreams is a huge component of our big picture happiness. Our life dreams begin at an early age. And when we get the chance to make them come to life, when we can live our dreams, we find great satisfaction and happiness in both the achievement of our dreams and the experience of them. Realizing our dreams can challenge us in the process. Along our way to our dreams, make sure we take time out to celebrate our progress and keep our focus positive.

- **Stay grounded in your identity** and do things that make you feel energized and empowered to be your best you.
- **Be the solution**—don't allow blame and judgment to be part of your conversation as they drag us down and prevent us from living our dreams. Just seek constructive, positive solutions that will keep you moving forward and growing.

3. Accountability

As with all goals, we need a plan to realize our dreams. Create a series of steps that you can start taking to make your dream a reality. You may not know all the steps when you begin, but you have to start the process. Begin with the steps you can see you need to take and as you get farther along in the process, you will know better what your next steps are. Write a series of goals for yourself and make a daily commitment to dream time!

- Align yourself with the path to realize your dreams. Step by step, day by day. If you take even a tiny step forward each day, you keep your momentum going and your energy focused on achieving your dreams.

4. Gratitude
Realizing our dreams can seem to be a daunting, even unreachable goal. If we listen to our fears and our doubts, our dreams might well be unattainable. But fear is a very real and formidable foe. Most of us face some degree of fear daily. One of the tricks to get past potentially paralyzing stumbling blocks like fear is to focus on gratitude. What about the process of living towards your dreams are you grateful for? I imagine we're all thankful for the opportunity to move towards our dreams and to live our dreams. But if we look at the steps we're taking to get there, what about each step are we grateful for? When we center our thoughts on gratitude, there is no room for fear. And we move one step closer.

- Accept fear but don't let it paralyze you—move forward in spite of it. When the big picture seems overwhelming, ask yourself what one tiny step can you take towards your dream. Take it. Step by step, that thing you fear doesn't have power over you anymore. You are not a coward! Cowards don't realize their dreams. You are intrepid!

5. Love
- **Articulate what you love.** Speaking your dream and writing it down is a powerful tool in committing to your goal.
- Follow your **passion**.
- **Envision your ideal life**—imagine it vividly every morning, or better yet, create a vision board with

pictures you've torn from magazines that represent the life of your dreams. Being able to see, not just imagine, your dream life sets your whole being in the direction of making those images a reality.

Other Values That Will Help You Reach Your Goal of Realizing Your Dreams

1. Wisdom
On every momentous journey, we learn far more than we perhaps anticipated we would along the way. If we value wisdom—about ourselves and more universal truths—realizing our dreams is possibly one of the most illuminating journeys we can take. With every challenge and celebration in the process, we can learn amazing life lessons that will continue to benefit us the rest of our lives. If wisdom is a strong value for us, welcome the stretching out of our comfort zones and enjoy!

2. Meaningful Work
When we set our sights toward realizing our dreams, we typically are aiming for achieving something that is extraordinarily meaningful to us. When we value meaningful work, meaningful occupations, meaningful contributions, the work is a reward in itself. We are fed by what we contribute and produce. Keep that in mind when you are on your way but feel you are not yet there. The work we invest in realizing our dreams is the most meaningful we can invest.

A Few Practical Steps Towards Realizing Our Dreams

- Think of your comfort zone not just as a safe pleasant place but think of it more like a doughnut. Something that is tasty and delightful but also isn't as beneficial to you as something like a fruit smoothie. Realizing your dream often requires we stretch out of our routines and safety zones. Step out of your comfort zone daily. And instead of thinking that we are leaving our safe happy place when we do, think about the doughnut. We'll get flabby and doughy if we stay there. So stepping out, though it can feel a little nerve-racking, will ultimately make us feel happier and more energized…much like the smoothie.
- Focus, focus, focus. If our dream requires that we save money to go to school or to open our business or to travel (or whatever the case may be), keep that in our focus. When we see a great sale on the perfect pair of boots or flat screen TV or new car…do we really need that? Or is that tempting treasure merely a distraction from our goal? Keep your eyes on the prize and pass every temptation by the litmus test of whether it will unnecessarily cost us from getting closer to our dream.

Helpful Resources

1. Support system—use friends and family to keep us on our path. Sometimes we can get so enmeshed in the challenges we face along the way or in day-to-day that it's hard to keep our energy and enthusiasm aimed at realizing our dream. Our support system can remind us of why our dreams are so important to us and can cheer us on and get us through the challenges along the way.

2. Books and role models—sometimes we just need a little extra oomph to stay the course as we work towards our dreams. It helps me to read stories of other people who ultimately realized their dreams and to read of the frustrations and doubts as well as of the discoveries and delights along their path.

3. Internet—the Internet can be a powerful research tool in helping us to make educated choices as we move towards our dreams, and it can be a powerful connecting tool in finding others who have accomplished dreams similar to ours. Research and partners in dreams can go a long way in helping us reach our goals.

Personal Story: Listening to My Courage to Follow My Career Dreams

My first career out of college was that of a newspaper reporter, and eventually section editor, for a series of weekly papers in northern Virginia. I loved it. My college major was Psychology, but I had dreams of reporting and writing stories. Only, after two years, the written word wasn't enough for me. I wanted my stories to include sound and picture. I LOVED documentary films. My heart told me to quit and follow my dream. My head told me I was in a good spot and that I was crazy to make that leap.

Unbeknownst to me, on the day my editor was going to invite me to lunch to give me a raise and speak to me about revving up my career, I walked in that morning and resigned to attend summer film school in Maine.

Happy? Giddily so. I was following a strong pull. My inner guide was telling me this was the right thing to do. And I trusted that guide because it made me grin from ear to ear, despite all the unknowns surrounding my decision. I was quitting a job, moving out of my home, leaving my friends and my familiar stomping grounds, putting my belongings in storage, and traveling alone to a month of classes at the end of which I had no plan.

*Did I **love** myself? Even more so than when I was happily ensconced at my computer writing stories every week on the arts and entertainment beat. I loved that I believed in myself enough to take the leap and see what happened. I was totally energized by the possibilities.*

*Did I have **self-respect**? You bet! I would NOT have respected myself if I had let myself stay small at a job where I had plateaued. I felt the creative call to explore new horizons and I was ready to answer the call. I respected myself enough to follow that voice that urged me to take the next step. And yes, it was scary in some ways. But taking my first job at the newspaper had been scary, too. I knew it was time to stretch my courage a little further, along with my creative skills.*

*Was I **accountable** about my new venture? Absolutely. I had my financial ducks in a row. I had no debt. I had a cushion of money to support me while I was there. And after my class was through, I ended up staying to work at the school for the rest of the year. I made connections there that I maintain to this day. And as for my old job, yes, when I learned my editor was going to give me a raise and help me move to the next level as a writer, I had pangs of regret. But I knew this was a step I needed* *to take for me, and I made good on the commitment to myself.*

*Am I **grateful**? I still am. To this day, I look on that period in my life as a charmed period. I was in an environment where we breathed, ate, slept creativity. And that part of Maine was gorgeous, to boot. It was a place and a time where I felt empowered and energized. And I carry that with me today. Not to mention the skills I learned there that enabled me to shift gears professionally and get into film and video where I am still happily nestled today. Also, that couple of months gave me a cadre of friends with whom I am still in touch. It was a shared experience that made it easy to bond with housemates, classmates, and workmates. Now, more than 15 years later, these are still friends who know me very well. And who share the creative drive. It was a time and experience that continues to pay dividends on the investment we made there. And that leap that I took to shift careers before I had any experience in the profession I wanted to get into? That leap gives me the chutzpah even now to follow my inner guide when I hear it calling. Grateful? Unspeakably.*

What's more, if I hadn't trusted my courage to get me through that leap, I think the rest of my life decisions could have suffered. I would have shrunk from taking leaps, preferring to play it safe, staying with the familiar, opting to not take risks. But no risks, no fantastic rewards.

Even before I really gave thought to my values, much less recognized the Five-to-Be-Alive values, they steered me to follow my fabulous custom-fit life path.—Liz

Personal Story: Mid-Life Professional Shift—Creating a Career from a Childhood Dream:

The first camera I can remember calling my own was a Polaroid Land Camera. You remember Polaroids? The instant photos were spit out from the camera, you waited a while to let the image develop, then you peeled away the cover to reveal… the magic of Polaroid. I loved shooting all our family gatherings… and my dog, and the snow, and the turtle in our backyard. You get the picture, I think. I was snap-happy.

I decided to leave my first job out of college, a newspaper reporter, to go to film school so I could add pictures and sound to the stories I was telling. Almost two decades later, I have come back to my roots as a shutterbug. I LOVE shooting. It gives me immense pleasure to capture life with my lens and share it with people.

I enjoy a career that keeps me energized and creatively challenged. I write books, scripts, and print materials, and I produce for film, broadcast corporate clients. And one of my dreams is to grow my career into documentary photography. It means taking a huge leap of faith and making a significant investment of time, energy and money on my part. But then, following dreams usually does involve such leaps.

Pursuing dreams is something we can all relate to. Achieving them is an entirely different matter. Achieving dreams, in my experience, comes only with the added and steadfast commitment to our Five-to-Be-Alive Values.

For this dream, I've begun the process, but it is still very much a work in progress. My roadmap for achieving my dream to be a documentary photographer is quite simple. I have outlined it here as an example of how we can all structure our blueprints for our dreams:

Sharing my photography brings me great joy. Schoolboys in Laos LOVED seeing their photos!

Step one: Love. Love on multiple levels, that is. First, photography is one of my passions. The process brings me joy and sharing the outcome with others brings me joy. Second, I love myself. How easy is it to admit that to ourselves? It may not have been as easy for me once as it is now. It is not a selfish statement. Quite the opposite. If I didn't love myself and take care of myself the way I would anyone else I love, I would have nothing to give to those dear to me.

Step two: **Happiness**. When I do things that make me happy, I radiate happiness and I can spread that with everyone I interact with and with everything I do. Happiness, do I have to say it? Happiness is essential. Does anyone really want misery over happiness? Happiness not only breeds health, satisfaction, love, all manner of levels of well-being, but that generally translates into professional and personal vitality.

*Step three: **Self-Respect**. I know, from experience, that as an artist, when I ignore, repress, dismiss my dreams and creative flow, I am in essence denying my gifts and potential contributions to the world. We all, after all, have gifts and contributions to share with the world. I will always choose to believe that my dreams are important and possible, choose to pursue my talents and gifts in the hope that somehow they will matter. To deny those entrenched allegiances to myself would be to deny my essence, my spirit, my purpose, my self. I don't see any good coming from that path.*

*Step four: **Gratitude**. Every day I feel lucky and grateful that I have dreams and passions that I am able to pursue. I can't imagine a life without them. They give me fire and direction and hope. And I am thankful for a life rich with possibility.*

*Step five: **Accountability**. Just articulating my love of photography and declaring my intention of being a documentary or street-style photographer isn't enough to make my dream a reality. Nope. A lot of sweat equity is in order. And to that end, I practice the accountability aspect of my path by putting my time, energy and money towards my dream. Specifically, I take photography courses, study photography books and blogs, spearhead a photography group that creates regular challenges and then critiques of our work, I shoot almost every day, and I have purchased a professional camera body and lenses. I am constantly striving to test my skills, hone my eye, understand how I see, push myself stylistically and explore new topics and methods in my documentary practice. Once I build my street portrait portfolio and attain a certain comfort level with creative and technical solutions to typical issues that arise when shooting,*

I will market myself as a street/documentary portrait photographer and go from there.

This is my ongoing roadmap for any challenge I set out for myself. The Five-to-Be-Alive values offer consistent guidelines to not only get us to our dreams, but to maintain those dreams once we achieve them. —Liz

Your Five-to-Be-Alive for Better Relationships

1. Self-Respect

Self-respect is important in every relationship you have. It helps ensure that you will not be taken advantage of; that you will be treated respectfully by others. If you do not know how to respect yourself then you might be subject to being disrespected, mistreated or exploited by others. There are at least two people in every relationship and it requires a commitment to the relationship to keep it in a positive, productive, mutually beneficial state. You have to contribute to that commitment by showing a respect to the other person but most importantly you have to enter into that relationship feeling sure of yourself; confident in yourself; understanding your self-worth and respecting yourself. This will allow you to optimize the relationships you choose to have in your life or those over which you have less control, such as relationships at your workplace or at your child's school. Having a healthy self-respect will assist you in recognizing when a relationship is becoming or has become one-sided, abusive or destructive. Your self-respect will give you the courage to voice your dissatisfaction or disapproval with those types of relationships or to walk away from them.

2. Happiness

A goal for everything you do should include being happy. What point is there to having a relationship with someone, anyone, if that person does not make you happy? Whether you are just starting a relationship with someone or are smack dab in the middle of one, your mutual happiness is of great importance. You don't have to be everything to everyone or vice versa.

Sometimes our relationships are complex where we share many interests and/or spend much time with that other person. Other times, our relationships happen because of circumstance—they are coincidental or accidental. We have relationships with coworkers, with parents of our children's friends, with neighbors and community members. Sometimes these relationships end up being temporary—when whatever brought people together goes away, sometimes the relationship does too. Whatever the nature of your relationship, be it a close bond with someone or a more coincidental, situational type of thing, you should do everything in your power to ensure the connections and interactions you have are happy ones.

3. Accountability

One might think that being accountable in relationships depends on the type of relationship you have but that's not really true. Relationships, regardless of the type, are about give and take; they involve at least two people, so to be accountable to your relationship you have to be thinking of more than just yourself. Whether it's a work relationship or a personal friendship or something related to your community in some way, being accountable pretty much means the same thing. If someone is counting on you for something (which happens all the time in relationships) then you need to deliver. If you say you are going to do something, do it. If you say you're going to be somewhere at a certain time, be there. If you are running late or can't make an appointment, call the person who is waiting for you. Keep your word. Meet your deadlines. Show up. Be the person they expect you to be. You can tailor these directives to meet whatever the scenario is—meeting a friend for lunch, taking the dog for a walk, being at a business meeting, helping out at a school function. When you are in a relationship there are expectations of some sort so meet or exceed them. That's being accountable to those with whom you are in a relationship.

4. Gratitude

Don't forget to express appreciation to those people you have relationships with: spouses, significant others, bosses, coworkers, subordinates, bus drivers, teachers, neighbors, friends, children, family, doctors, coaches, fellow club members, babysitters, veterinarians—everyone you have ongoing interactions with, basically. If you let people know that you care, that you are grateful to have them in your life—whether it's because you love them or because they take care of your children or pets when they are sick—if they know they are appreciated it will make them feel good, helpful and happy. This can only enhance your relationship and the interactions you have within that relationship. Expressing gratitude can result in more cordial exchanges, a closer bond to those you love, a sense of peace or assurance with oneself regarding the kind of job they are doing or service they are delivering. Gratitude lets people know that they are doing good stuff and that you have noticed which most likely will result in more of the same behaviors since they are being positively reinforced.

5. Love

We do not love every person with whom we have a relationship, and we would not suggest that that is a requirement. What you have to love, however, is what you get out of the relationship or the relationship itself. If you are in a book club, you may love the meetings where you get together and talk about the book you read. If you are a classroom volunteer, you may love working with the children or the feeling you get from helping out. If you have friends, you may love how they make you laugh or like the same kinds of movies as you or how you can talk until the wee hours of the morning and never run out of things to say. What can help you have better relationships is that understanding: knowing what it is you love about them. Whether it's the people themselves or certain traits of the people or a combination of the people and the activities you share with them—knowing what it is you love about these relationships is important to keeping them on sure ground and getting the very most out of them. You may love having coffee with a certain friend but you may not enjoy going to movies with her. Even with relationships we don't choose—like those we have with coworkers. It may take a little more work or a change in thinking to get to what you love about those relationships, but if you take the time to go through the exercise it will give you that positive to focus on. Make it easy—find one trait about someone with whom you work that you like. Maybe someone is friendly, even if they are a slacker. Maybe someone is smart as a whip, even if she doesn't return your calls in a timely manner. Maybe someone is very thorough, even if they are a little slower in getting tasks done.

Sometimes if you focus on the relationship in a bigger picture way, that can help you, too. Maybe look at your relationship with work—maybe you love the challenge of your job, or the salary, or the nature of the work you do—whatever it is that you love, figure out how to fold the relationships into it. Your co-workers are a part of that big picture so if you allocate a little love of that job to them, giving them a little credit for it, then you will find that you can improve those relationships in the process. In all the relationships we have there is some kind of love involved so find it and understand it, and you will be able to direct your focus to it. That can only have positive results.

Other Values That Will Help You Have Better Relationships

1. Honesty

Relationships fail when the people involved are not honest with one another. Friendships have been dissolved over lies. Corporations have fallen. Be honest in your relationships.

2. Forgiveness

People will make mistakes, forget an appointment or a meeting. You can express your dissatisfaction, but people in relationships forgive one another, especially when the shortfall is not habitual.

3. Generosity

A show of support goes a long way. There are many ways to give, to be generous to those with whom we have relationships. We can lend an ear, we can show up when called upon to do so, we can put the other person first. We can be generous in our words and our actions towards the people with whom we have relationships. If something is needed, we can do what we can to provide it.

4. Civility

One of the most important values you can practice in relationships is civility. Being kind, respectful and polite in your discourse is the only way to be if you want your relationships to remain strong and intact. Losing your cool or becoming rude does nothing but cause hurt or angry feelings, at a minimum, and takes the relationship down a negative path.

5. Patience

Everyone is different; remember there is more than one approach to most things. Finding the right dynamic in a relationship takes time, relationships have to be nurtured. Change and growth doesn't happen overnight, they don't call it "building relationships" for nothing.

A Few Practical Steps for Achieving Better Relationships

1. Communicate.
- If you are a party in a relationship, do not "shut down." Relationships are a two-way street and so is communication.
- Speak your mind. Nothing can change or improve if you don't share what's on your mind.
- Relationships cannot succeed or flourish if those involved don't talk to one another about their needs and wants.

2. Get out of the house or office.
- Sometimes relationships need a change of venue. Get out and find someplace new to talk or work things out.
- Ruts can get formed with routines, if you feel your relationship is waning or in need of a boost, change up your routine.

3. Schedule time to work on your important relationships.
- Don't use being busy as an excuse for ignoring important relationships.
- Proactively plan and schedule to be with people in your important, meaningful relationships. This will help keep them fresh, comfortable and sound.

4. Put the other person first.
- Don't be selfish. Don't always insist that it be your way.
- Think of what the other person or people would want and put those wants ahead of your own if they differ.
- Remember that relationships are about "we" not "me."

5. See a therapist or counselor.

- If you can't resolve issues or are unhappy with an important relationship, such as your spouse or your children, seek outside help.
- Recognize that you can lose clarity when emotions are involved and an outsider may be able to offer a new, unbiased and/or helpful perspective.

All of the above practical steps are simply suggestions that may help you have better relationships. Relationships can be complicated; some carry painful baggage; some affect our earning potential; all affect our quality of life. It's important to think about what you want out of your relationships and think about ways to get what you want, always remembering that it needs to be mutually beneficial, that it has to be best for the relationship, not just you.

Helpful Tips/Resources

1. Web sites
There are too many web sites to list but if you do a search on relationships, better relationships or something more specific about relationships you will get back more results that you can ever get through. It might take time to get to what you are looking for but if you like to use the Internet as a resource you will be able to find advice or information that may help.

2. Books/Publications
There are myriad books about how to have better relationships—some are broad-reaching, others talk about specific types of relationships. Depending on your interest and/or need you may find the information in some of these books to be useful.

3. Friends

We are in relationships with our friends. They can sometimes see in us things we miss about ourselves. Ask them to be honest with you about what you can do to be a better friend or a better party in a relationship. You will need thick skin for this but it can pay off if it is thoughtful, actionable information.

4. Family

Ditto with our family. Our families often know us best—warts and all. It could be useful to know what they think those warts are so we can get rid of them!

Personal Story: Making Travel with Family a Priority

Some people don't like to travel. It's a nuisance, a pain, a hassle. Not me, I love it! Even though it can indeed be a hassle I can't imagine not being able to get away and experience new places. It's almost a need that must be fed. It is a passion I want to pass down to my children if that's possible. I want them to have these experiences and provide them the opportunities if we can; show them as much of the world as we can—whether it is someplace an hour's drive away or takes many hours on a plane to get there.

I was not well-traveled as a child. I didn't miss that, for you can't miss what you haven't done, it is just something we didn't do growing up. I honestly can't remember there being time for it. But when I saw photographs of pretty places or what I thought were interesting places I do recall having that feeling of "I'd like to visit there" but it wasn't a yearning. When I was 16 years old, however, the yearning began. I took a trip that was offered through my high school to Spain. I was done for after that. I was in love. I was awe-struck and moved by things that I saw. The sheer beauty of a place was enough to cause that effect but then there were the buildings and the amazement that came from simply knowing how old a structure was and how impossible it seemed that something so grand and intricate could have been built many hundreds of years ago without the assistance of modern equipment. It was then that I knew travel would become a priority if I could afford it.

Prior to going to Spain my sister and I had some very memorable and hilarious trips with our grandmother, two great aunts and a great uncle. They took us to Florida, Niagara Falls and Williamsburg. These trips were priceless because of the people we were with. The trips themselves were great but when we talk about those times it's always things that happened with our relatives or situational things that we recall. We laugh so hard we almost cry. We saw our relatives in a different light when we were out of "real life" and on vacation. It was all about the being together and doing stuff of interest together. Meals weren't routine like they might be at home, they were events. Everything you did was part of the vacation. This aspect of traveling appealed to me and is part of why I wanted to have family vacation experiences as much as our schedules and bank account would allow. When you get away from the daily grind you are able to detach from that work, those chores and be able to focus on those you are with 100%, you can connect more. There is no laundry to be done, no dishes to be rinsed out in the sink (unless you're at a beach house but it's still different), no practices, lessons, etc. you have to get to. You are there together to be together.

When I stopped working and our income basically was cut in half we had to become very mindful of spending and saving. Gone were the days of saying "oh look, there's a sale on flights to wherever, let's go." My husband and I had done some traveling before we had children and, for a couple of years when our son was small, still took trips, just the two of us. It, of course, became more complicated and more expensive to add the cost of one more person and then two when our daughter came along. The number of trips and the types of places we visited changed. My husband and I were actually at odds on this topic. I still wanted to travel, to take all our extra money and put it towards trips whereas my husband was more conservative, more responsible, really, and wanted to put it away for the unexpected home or car repair. I, however, continued to look online at locations, travel deals and would pitch things to him for every four-day weekend the kids had or Spring Break or summer vacation. It was always a priority on paper but not always in actuality. And sometimes when we did travel we'd back off from where we really wanted to go and settle for something less expensive because "that made sense."

I'm not sure when the mindset changed but it was something my husband and I had to do together. Together we had to figure out how to make traveling as a family a priority—not so easy when you look at it from a feasibility standpoint—financially, fitting it into our busy schedules, ensuring our travel plans do not interfere with the commitments we and our children have made to others or with anything else that is important, necessary or should come first. But what happened is that there came a point when we said, in effect, that we only live once, that our kids will be young and living with us for only so long so now is the time to travel and have those experiences with them. Will it mean retirement comes a little later because we aren't stashing that money away? Maybe, but this is something we wanted to do. It's something we wanted to experience now and later, not just later.

I am still the one who has to be the motivator for these family trips. My husband readily admits to being a half-empty glass on travel until we are actually on the trip then he is 100% into it and glad we're there. For us to get to making this a priority we had to come to a meeting of the minds and also recognize our differing personalities, approach and mindset relative to it. In relationships it's give and take. In many ways we were at opposite ends of the spectrum—my wanting to travel as much as possible and he, while not being opposed to travel, usually felt that money should be saved for emergencies, that unexpected but unavoidable expense. I would find myself at times not bothering to bring up taking a trip, knowing how he felt, and there were times when he likely agreed to trips when he felt a bit wary of spending the money. It required an openness on both our parts to find the right middle ground—to make it a priority, but to remember some flexibility may be needed.

In a nutshell we were able to make travel with family a priority by:

- *Opening up the communication lines between my husband and me*
- *Compromising. Destinations, costs, travel dates, length of trip and other factors had to be considered in order to not end up at an impasse.*

- Setting aside or saving the money needed for these trips.
- Understanding and agreeing upon why these travel experiences are important from a relationship standpoint, not just wanting to see a new place or get away.

This goal was important to me because I love to experience new places. I also love being with my family

Being able to share her love of and the experience of travel with her family is a profound source of gratitude for Amy.

and experiencing the unique connections we have when we travel. I feel much gratitude towards our Earth and I never tire of getting to see parts of it. I want to take it all in or as much of it as possible for it makes me feel connected to it—to the Earth and all those who live on it. I needed to understand, inside, why travel was important to me, why it was important to share with my family. It is more than just taking a trip and swimming in a hotel pool 500 miles from home. It is more than just getting away from the every day routines of home life. It is more than just seeing a pretty place or experiencing a new town. It is about love and gratitude for me. My life, my capacity to love and to feel grateful, is enhanced by our travel experiences. This is the true reason why and what drove me to make travel with my family a priority and what kept me from giving up on that reality. —Amy

Your Five-to-Be-Alive for Career/Work Improvements

1. Self-Respect

If you don't have confidence in yourself how can you expect those that work for you to have confidence in you? Those who don't have a healthy self-esteem, who are not confident in themselves, will instill doubt in others. Coworkers will not turn to you for help. Supervisors won't recommend you for promotions. You need to "walk tall" and hold your head up high at your place of business. When it's called for, assert yourself. If you can handle it, ask for more responsibility. Always show people through your words and actions that you are able to do your job well—be someone that people would describe as "going places." Knowing what you are worth—not just monetarily—is important in the job market. Yes, you are worth your salary but you are worth and deserve much more—people owe you respect, civility, honesty and appreciation. If you don't respect yourself you will not get any of those things in return and will have difficulty making the changes you want to make or reaching the professional goals that you have.

2. Happiness

Don't be the office grump. You know the ones, they don't look people in the eye, seem 'put out' when you interact with them, they seem unapproachable, people avoid them. They don't exude happiness. Maybe they aren't happy. Either way, it is off-putting. People tend to want to work with and interact with people who have a happy demeanor. Being happy with your job is important to your personal well-being, but it plays a role in whether you will be able to make positive changes in your workplace. If you are happy, people will want to be a part of your team—you will not be viewed as confrontational. People will assume that you will be more agreeable to deal with in times of stress and less likely to be unpleasant to work with. Perceptions are important to getting buy-in. If someone has a positive perception of you they will likely be more open with you from the onset, more likely to compromise or agree over work issues that crop up. Likeability is important—in some jobs more than others—happy people are more likeable. How you are perceived by others in your workplace impacts how happy your workplace is for you. You can help ensure happiness on the job by seeking out employment that allows you to do things you enjoy, feel challenged by or that give you the opportunity to make a difference. Then by sharing that happy demeanor at the office you contribute to a more positive, pleasant environment. You can't control how happy others are, but you can do whatever you can to be happy yourself and to pass that onto others—it can play a role in your mood at work and at home and improve your quality of life.

3. Accountability

Accountability may be the most important of the Five-to-Be-Alive to improve your status in the office. If people can't depend on you then you're going nowhere, you may not even keep your job. If coworkers, supervisors, clients, vendors and/or anyone else with whom you interact with your job cannot rely on you to follow through on your commitments or meet your job criteria, you have little hope of doing anything more than what you are presently doing and may be risking demotion or being let go. It's pretty simple. Do the job you are supposed to be doing. Don't miss deadlines or, if you are going to, make appropriate people aware. Ask for help when you need it. Call people back. Communicate as needed. Keep your customers happy—internal and external. Admit your mistakes. Fix what you break. Take credit when it's due but give it to others when it should be given. Show up and let your word be your bond. Walk your talk.

4. Gratitude

Be grateful for the job that you have simply because you have work, you are employed. Find what it is that you appreciate about it and remind yourself regularly to be grateful, to appreciate those aspects of your work. Even if you aren't in your dream job or exactly where you want to be, be grateful for where you are at any given moment, even as you work to be or want to be someplace else. Be aware of what you do appreciate and keep your focus on it—think big and think small. Be grateful for the salary (even if you think it's too low—and we all think our salaries are too low—it's still money and it's still helping provide for ourselves and our families). Be grateful to not be idle, to not be unemployed, to be contributing to society—whether you're working the drive-thru window at a fast food restaurant or in the management or executive ranks of a large corporation, you are filling a need, you are contributing to our economy. Be grateful for challenges, the opportunities to find solutions to problems. Be grateful to be able to interact with other people, to maybe add to their day in a positive way. Be grateful for chit-chat in the break room; the camaraderie you develop with coworkers; the opportunity to learn new things; the way someone greets you each day. There are so many things that happen in the course of our work day, so many things that we are exposed to and are doing. We may not be happy about or appreciate them all but there are always things for which we can be appreciative when it comes to our jobs. At the very least we need to remember that we are being a contributor to something when we work. That whatever we are doing is allowing us to earn a living.

5. Love

Is there love in business? Sounds kind of strange but some people do love their jobs. They have a passion for whatever it is they are doing. Like any kind of love, that just sort of happens, it develops. You can certainly seek out jobs that you think you'll like or love and once in them that passion may develop and you'll be one of those lucky ones who love their job. There are things, though, that can help you fall in love with your job. They include: having a positive attitude, being open to the opinions of others, taking in all the wisdom and knowledge—learning as much as you can from coworkers, being civil and encouraging civility in your work environment, looking at everything as an opportunity or a learning experience, being grateful and determined. Some days you'll have a love for your job and others not so much. When you have those days of loving your job, stop and think about what it is that made you feel that way and make a conscious effort to repeat or replicate what you can on a regular basis. Do the same on those not-so-good days. Figure out what it was that made it such a bad day and, with those things you can control, learn from them and do everything you can to avoid them in the future. Another way of looking at love in business is by showing it to others—by sharing your knowledge, empowering other people, sharing contacts, strategies and anything else that help others be successful. It also means being kind, empathetic, tolerant and understanding to and of those with whom you work. These examples of love—be it loving your job or extending "love" to others in the business world—can improve your outlook regarding work and when noticed will increase your opportunities for advancement at work.

Other Values For Achieving Work or Career Path Improvements

1. Civility

You must be able to get along with others to be successful at work. Being civil sometimes means holding your tongue or taking a conversation offline. Showing respect for those with whom you work is civil behavior that should be a no-brainer.

2. Integrity

Do everything with integrity. Being honest and ethical in your work, delivering a quality product or service and showing respect for those around you is one way to do your job with integrity. There will always be critics of the job you have done or the deliverable you have created but leave no doubt as to whether you have exhibited integrity as you've done that job or produced that deliverable.

3. Patience

Everyone works at a different pace and follows his own process to get the job done. Recognize that you cannot expect others to march to the same drumbeat that you do. Show patience and tolerance for those differing approaches from coworkers.

4. Determination

Some jobs take more determination than others. Work with a purpose. Be resolved to meet or exceed the expectations that are set for or by you. When you are under the gun or faced with challenges, determination is required to keep you going until you see the job through. Giving up is not an option. Redesigning or forming a new approach is not giving up—they are different paths that a determined person may take to get to the required end result.

5. Perseverance

Perseverance and determination go hand in hand. If determination is strength of mind to see something through, perseverance would be what turns that determination into a concrete result. To persevere one must keep trying even after you've been met by failure; you don't let the problem or the task get the best of you. It requires courage, tenacity and endurance to keep doing what needs to be done to reach the final goal.

A Few Practical Steps for Making Career/Work Improvements

1. Network.
- Take the time to get to know your coworkers in the office.
- Spend time outside of the office with coworkers.

2. Increase or take advantage of educational opportunities.
- Take courses that will aid you in being more effective, productive or knowledgeable in your field of work.
- Participate in in-house training that is made available to you.

3. Use a scheduling system.
- Figure out what works best for you to maintain an organized state at the office.
- Use tools that will assist you in tracking and meeting deadlines and appointments.
- Make sure you plan in advance to avoid being overbooked.

4. Be generous with your knowledge and time.
- Don't hide information that will help others be successful at work or that will increase the probability of success for the organization.
- Recognize that enabling others to succeed is a success itself.
- Share what you have learned, take the time to help or train others.

5. Ask for help.
- When you are in over your head, ask for help. Being accountable means recognizing your limitations.
- If you are unsure of what is expected of you, ask for clarification.
- If you do not feel you can meet or exceed the expectations of a task due to lack of knowledge, understanding, time or other reason, request assistance.

All of the above practical steps are simply suggestions that may help you reach your work/career improvement goals. Depending on your job you may have small goals or big goals. They may be financial in nature or relate more to being fulfilled on a personal level. Whatever the case may be, the requirements for making those improvements are the same, they just may be more involved with some careers or jobs than with others. It is important to recognize what you want to get out of your job or career and always work towards that goal. If your goal is fulfillment, don't take a position that doesn't meet that goal. It may require taking the money piece of it out of the equation so as not to muddy the waters. Money is nice and will pay the bills but it is not what makes a job or career fulfilling or meaningful.

Helpful Tips/Resources

1. Web sites
- www.career-advice.monster.com/
- www.careers.org/

2. Books/Publications
Check out the career/jobs section at your local library or bookstore.

3. Friends
- Human Resources is your friend. Seek advice from the HR resources at your office. Part of their job is career development and employee guidance. Plus you can ensure confidentiality—that is also part of their job.
- Ask your friends to tell you your best personality traits and your worst. Ask them what you think might make it difficult to work with you. Thick skin is again required.

4. Family
- Family members may have connections to people in businesses you want to be in. Ask them if they will help you get in the door.
- Anyone who has a job or job experience may have useful advice. Be willing to listen.

5. The Internet
Search to your heart's content. There's lots of information out there.

Personal Story: Focusing on Fulfilling Work

When my daughter was six months old and my son halfway through kindergarten I quit my job. My six-figure income was no more. On the one hand it was a very easy decision but on the other it was incredibly difficult—not just to make but to accept over time.

The term "golden handcuffs" is one that I had heard used over the years and I had come to understand exactly what that meant. In order for me to be able to resign from my job I had to take the money out of the equation. It had to be about doing what was right for me and my family on a personal level. I had achieved a decent amount of success professionally and knew I could continue to be successful. This was appealing to me but not if it was at the expense of what my husband and I felt was best for our family. My income, while not required to make ends meet, certainly was of benefit. It made life more comfortable—and the security of having a second income brought peace of mind as well. In the end, however, the decision was a seemingly easy one to make. I didn't feel we could be the best parents we could be with us both working or at least not with us both working the kinds of jobs we were doing. The decision became one of either my working part-time or not working at all. I chose to not work at all. Well, sort of. That was eight years ago (at the time of this writing).

Not long after I quit this job I was working again and have continued to do so ever since. Nothing full-time and nothing that has really interfered with our family life. I still often say that I don't work when I'm asked because sometimes it's sort of hard to explain. I've done many things for the last eight years—all of which have been fulfilling, none of which, as of yet, has been particularly lucrative. I have worked for my husband's company assisting in various capacities where I've gotten to use my business experience and skills. I've taught Spanish classes to elementary-aged children and tutored high school students in the language. And I've been General Manager of a company whose focus is on reinforcing the practice of positive values. All of these efforts have been very fulfilling for me. My corporate, high-paying jobs were very fulfilling too, but they did not allow me the flexibility to be with my children in the way that these other jobs have which, it turns out, has been of significant importance.

Over the years I have had opportunities to reenter the workforce in a full-time capacity doing work like I did before. It has been difficult to pass on those opportunities. I did enjoy working and of course the extra income was nice but I could never reconcile having a full-time job and being able to participate in my children's lives in the way that I wanted. One thing I knew I needed, however, was some kind of job or commitments that felt like work. This was in addition to all the work I was doing being a parent and running a household. It wasn't something I had to be paid for but it was something I needed. What I did was seek out volunteer opportunities within my children's schools. These were rewarding for me, and my children felt good about my being involved. I didn't really seek out any paid position, all of the paying jobs I've had in the past eight years have sort of found me. My husband's company approached me, the Spanish job sort of fell into my lap after a summer Spanish camp my son participated in, the tutoring engagements were requested by people who knew me and my Spanish abilities and the values work I've been doing was presented to me by a relative. One thing all of these jobs have had in common is that they are all fulfilling. I have enjoyed doing all of them and have continued to pursue opportunities with all of them because of the satisfaction they bring, not the money.

I have been fortunate and am quite grateful to be in the position to do work that may not be financially lucrative but out of which I derive great satisfaction. I have choices that many do not have and I do not take that good fortune for granted. I appreciate it immensely. I feel good about what I can contribute to the work I do, to the people or companies for whom I work. When one of my kindergarteners tells me they love coming to Spanish class, that is more valuable to me than any paycheck. When people tell me that the work I'm doing with values is good and important work, it keeps me going and wanting to do more. When I see the value I add to a business opportunity through the bits of work I do with my husband's company I feel good about helping. I love being busy. Sometimes I'll say I hate it but I don't really. It overwhelms me sometimes but I can't imagine not having a lot to do.

Something I have had to accept is that I am not contributing to the household in a way that is allowing us to make big financial gains. It is hard to accept this because I know that I could find another high-paying job that would make life easier in many ways, that would more quickly increase the balances of those college and retirement funds. I have felt, for that reason, I am not doing all that I could for my family. At the same time, however, I know that it would likely make life more complicated. We are giving up money in order for me to be more available to our children. To replace that money I might have to give up things on which you cannot put a price tag—seeing my children grow up and being as involved in their lives as I can be. It might seem easy, then, to make the choice, but it has not always been that way. My kids would not suffer if I went back to working full time. I know they'd be fine. I did work for the first five-and-a-half years of my son's life so I know first-hand that it can work. I've also seen countless dual-income families make it work and their children bear no scars from it. Regardless of how I've looked at it and how comfortable I've been with my choice, I have had this internal battle for years. What I've determined is that it's actually impossible to resolve, I've just had to come to terms with my choices.

*What I eventually learned was that I have a **responsibility** to myself and to my family to pursue what is ultimately best for us all; what will make everyone **happiest**. Perhaps not perfectly happy or ideally happy but the happiest we can be when everything has been taken into consideration. My focus had to be on being fulfilled, on being satisfied and on being happy. If I am not these things then what good am I to my family? I had to recognize that my **self-worth** was not defined by a paycheck; that I should not **respect myself** more or less based on what my income was (or wasn't). When I took into consideration the responsibility I felt towards my family and my home, the **love** I have for my family and then added in the happiness factor, I realized that doing fulfilling work was more important than making a lot of money. I am very **grateful** that my husband is able to provide enough income for our family so that I have this choice. Knowing that I am doing things that I enjoy, that are contributing to the betterment of others, that make me happy and make me a better person towards those I love has allowed me to move past the fact that I am not a breadwinner in this household. I am paid more in laughs, smiles, words of thanks, hugs, and good feelings than I am with dollars and cents. This is truly more than enough.—Amy*

Your Five-to-Be-Alive for Finding/Preserving Love

1. Self-Respect

You can't be expected to find or even recognize real love if you don't have any or enough self-respect. People with low self-esteem or self-respect can easily confuse other expressions as being love when they are not. Lust or physical desire often gets mistaken for love. Someone must love all that you have to offer, not just your physical beauty or being. Some think being showered with gifts means they are loved. Material things, pretty things are nice and they may come from someone who truly loves you, but love is not seen in something you wear or hold in your hands. Some think that the angrier or the more jealous a significant other gets means they must really love them otherwise why would they be so upset, so passionately covetous? You have to have self-respect to recognize the differences between real love and that which is masquerading as love. You have to be confident in yourself to know why you should be loved—what makes you loveable. It is not that you have a pretty neckline for that pendant he bought you; it is not that you so physically attractive that you arouse passion in him; it is not because you are able to incense him with jealousy and/or anger over what you do or don't do. You need to know that you deserve respect, kindness, compassion, understanding and trust from someone who loves you; that you are more than just what one sees on the outside and that you are to be loved for all that you offer, for all that you are.

2. Happiness

Being in love should make you happy. If it doesn't, then it's not love or it's not the right love for you. Some people fall in love but cannot and do not have successful relationships. This happens. Not all people who are in love can live together, can agree on how to have a life together or share enough interests to be a couple forever. It's heartbreaking but it happens. Being in love is not always enough. If you make someone else happy and he makes you happy you are on your way to finding love and having it stick around after you do. It's important to remember that the *person* is the one to make you happy, not all the *stuff* around that person. Does s/he make you smile, laugh, feel good inside no matter where you are or what you are doing? It's pretty easy to feel happiness cruising in the Caribbean or people-watching in Paris, but don't confuse your happiness with where you are and what you are doing with being happy with the person you are with. Most of us can be happy in the tropics or a romantic European city with just about anyone but you need to ask yourself if you can be happy with that person in normal, everyday life. Would you be happy with that person just watching TV, cooking dinner, tending to mundane chores, hanging out? Can you be happy with that person if you are living paycheck to paycheck? It's important to remember to keep people and circumstances separate. No one wants to live paycheck to paycheck but if you are doing it with someone who truly makes you happy then you are lucky (even if not rich). And cruising down the Seine can be romantic and wonderful and make you feel happy, but don't let the view around you confuse you into thinking that guy or gal sitting next to you really does it for you. If the feelings you have for someone don't include happiness then you may not find love with that person. And if someone stops making you happy, love might have left or be on its way out. Happiness is a key ingredient in loving, lasting relationships.

3. Accountability

In any sort of relationship where love is involved the stakes are high—the pain of a broken heart is like no other pain. Being accountable in a relationship with a significant other or spouse means being honest; doing what you say you are going to do; apologizing or taking responsibility when you don't follow through or when you hurt another's feelings; communicating; contributing to the relationship—emotionally, physically, financially and/or in any other way that you have agreed to do; admitting fault; helping to solve differences; compromising; being in the thing together. When you are in love being accountable means you have to think of the person you love in whatever you are doing.

4. Gratitude

Be grateful and appreciative of the ones you love. There are few things worse than feeling taken for granted or marginalized in a relationship. One mustn't openly express thanks for every little thing, but the absence of gratitude—either verbal or non-verbal—may leave the parties in a relationship feeling unappreciated which can lead to feelings of being unwanted or unneeded or unloved. Make sure you show your gratitude for the ones you love, make sure they know what they mean to you, that you appreciate them, that they mean something to you, that their just being in your life is important to you and your well-being.

5. Love

Well, it goes without saying that to find and/or preserve love you must be able to love. Yourself and whoever that special person is whom you love or are looking to love. Loving another involves many emotions, feelings and values—it encompasses caring for that person, empathizing, sympathizing, a desire to please him, to share, to experience, to support, to just be together. You have to open your heart—all the way, not just a notch—to truly love someone. You have to be brave, vulnerable and trusting. It's a big deal. In order to find and keep love you have to be open to so much more than just caring about that person. There are many flavors of love, but the one that comes for that special someone, that soul mate (if you believe in the idea of a soul mate), that person with whom you think you can spend the rest of your life, is an all-encompassing emotion that requires you to let the other person in, to put down that wall and say "yes" to all of the above. We don't advise that you become blinded by this love of yours such that you lose rational thought, mind you, but you do have to have an openness like no other when you are looking for love, in love and trying to hold onto it forever.

Other Values For Finding/Preserving Love

1. Honesty

Tell the truth, even when it's not what the other person

wants to hear. Be yourself: don't try to be what you think others want you to be. Don't hide or withhold important information.

2. Generosity

Give to your partner of yourself—give your time, your love, your smiles, your kindness. Don't keep score. Be generous, giving in every way you can to show how much the other person means to you.

3. Patience

Love usually does not happen at first sight. Understanding takes patience. Compromise takes patience. Going from 'like' to 'love' takes time. Not letting the little things get in the way or turn into big things requires patience.

4. Kindness

When dealing with easy or difficult challenges use kind words, be compassionate, be sympathetic. You may cause irreversible damage to your relationship by being harsh, unfeeling or petty during disagreements or in times of strife.

5. Forgiveness

There will be bad days and stressful days when the worst comes out in us. Give a little. Forgive a little. Unexpected or out-of-character behaviors may crop up from time to time. When the apology comes, accept it. Don't make your partner "pay" an unreasonable price for their mistake or oversight.

A Few Practical Steps for Finding/Preserving Love

1. Be open.
- Don't withhold information or your feelings from the one you love.
- Honestly and respectfully share your likes/dislikes.
- Communicate how you feel about anything that can have an impact on your relationship.

2. Step out of your comfort zone.
- Have the courage to try new things—new food, traveling, sports, anything.
- Put the other person's interests/wants first and be willing to go with the flow.
- Speak up and take charge sometimes if you're usually quiet and easy-going; sit back and defer to your partner if you're usually the one who 'runs the show'.

3. Be creative.
- Don't get stuck in the same routine—be it with meals, sex, socializing, whatever—mix it up!
- Do something unexpected just for fun. Something small like sending a crazy or sexy e-card just because or taking the day off to do something fun or different together.

4. Learn to say "I'm sorry" and mean it.
- Apologize when you've hurt feelings or upset your partner. Be sincere.

- Remember that you may need to apologize for a situation or circumstance that has occurred even if you didn't cause it.
- Saying "I'm sorry" is an important and effective way to show empathy. It doesn't always have to be used to admit fault or take the blame for something.

5. Be adventurous.
- Be willing to let someone else make the decisions.
- Say 'yes' to those things you usually pass on.
- Seek out new and exciting things to do and do them.

All of the above practical steps are simply suggestions that may help you find love and/or maintain it.

Helpful Tips/Resources

1. Web sites*
- www.eHarmony.com

2. Books/Publications
- You may find advice or beneficial information in magazines or books relating to love and how to find, care and feed it.

3. Friends
- Ask friends to set you up on dates with people they know and with whom they think you'll be compatible.
- Double date or socialize with other married couples with whom you are friends.
- Go to events/places with friends where you may be able to meet people with like interests such as church, wine tastings, speaking events, dances, etc.

4. Family

- Ask family members to arrange dates with people with whom they think you'll be compatible.
- Encourage family members to make your significant other or spouse feel welcomed, accepted and a part of your family.

5. The Internet*
- Join a dating site like eHarmony.com
- Network/seek out relationships on social networking sites like Facebook.
- Join sites or discussion groups about things you are interested in.

We do not recommend or endorse any site listed. If you seek friendships or relationships via the Internet, be mindful to use credible sites that are secure, researched, professional and monitored. Do your homework and put your personal safety before all else.

Personal Story: The Journey of Loving Our Way Through Challenges

In January 2008, my aunt and I promised each other on my last visit to her before her death that month, that I would run the Vancouver marathon in May 2009 and that she would be there with me. We both shared a love of Vancouver, and as it might be apparent, we were quite special to each other.

For months I logged on to the marathon's website waiting for them to open their registration for 2009. Sometime in the summer, as soon as they allowed, I registered for the full marathon. Officially, my training schedule would begin in December, but I needed to have weeks of running in before that to build my weekly mileage base. Training is a delicate balance of steadily increasing weekly mileage while staying injury-free.

I knew travel plans were taking me out of running most of November so I ran for two months prior to my departure until I was at a good base mileage level. I thought I could pick back up pretty easily when I got home and be in good shape to start training in December.

Only, I got injured while I was away. And when I got home I ran twice and then couldn't run at all without the kind of pain that makes you turn around and go home within a block. I rested a week or two and tried again. Not good. I went to my miracle-working sports therapist in hopes she could get me back on the road without too much time lost. It took a couple visits before she found the problem. And once she did, it started improving immediately.

However, the biggest part of recovery is patience. Taking it slow. I was happy to stretch, roll on the deep tissue torture noodle, ice the injury, eat all the naturally anti-inflammatory foods I knew of, sleep more, all of it. But the patience was the toughest part. Every day I looked at my schedule and saw the training miles ramping up while I was still cooling my jets in the starting blocks.

I knew the big prize was the full marathon. But I had a goal to run a personal best at the age of 40 and to run this marathon in under 4 hours. That was going to require serious adherence to the training regimen. Miles and speed and miles and strength and, you guessed it, more miles. That's the training recipe for a sub-4 marathon. I needed to train. I needed to heal.

So how to stay in balance on my recovery? I looked to the Five-to-Be-Alive values for some wisdom and fortitude.

Love. *I was spilling over with love. Love for my aunt, love for running, love for marathon training, love for the kind of happy me I am when I am training, love for the adventure and challenge of setting a PR. But as my surgeon said to me when I recoiled upon seeing the stitches in my toe years ago, I must embrace my wound. My toe needed my love to heal. And now my body needed my love to heal. Instead of being agitated and irritated by being sidelined, I needed to and did embrace my leg as it was healing. I turned into a self-nurse giving my leg and body everything it could possibly need to get well and be strong. Love isn't just for when things are easy.*

Accountability. *I was committed to this marathon. I was committed to setting a PR if I could. But more importantly, I was going to run and I was going to raise money for ovarian cancer research in honor of my aunt. I would do whatever I could to keep myself healthy and sound so I would toe not just the starting line but the finish line.*

Self-Respect. *Instead of succumbing to doubt and anxiety and doom and gloom forecasts, every day I conjured images of myself running strong and sound through training and across the finish line. I researched all kinds of ways to bolster my body's ability to heal itself. I listened to my sports therapist's advice. I followed through on my therapy at home. I didn't give up. I didn't look for a way out. Instead, I worked harder mentally and physically in those weeks of recovery than I may have in training to stay focused and be as ready as I could* be to jump into training when I got the green light. This marathon was about love. And I was going to make good on my promise.

Happiness. Well, running makes me happy and I was having to stall the very practice that keeps me Zen and inspired. But happiness requires investment, too. Like love, it's not always an easy road. The balancing act is to find the happiness and the joy in every day, in the little moments. Particularly when life is frustrating and isn't going as planned. I knew there was gold in this injury hiatus and my recovery process. If anything, it only fortified my resolve to run this marathon and appreciation for being able to run. It made it more dear. And I was happy to be on the road to recovery. I was moving in a positive direction.

Gratitude. Every, and I cannot emphasize this enough, EVERY step I am able to run without pain, I am grateful for. Every run where I feel strong or have a-ha moments are icing on the cake. I am pig-in-slop happy to be able to run. I am grateful to my miracle-working sports therapist for making it possible. I am grateful to everyone who is supporting my fundraising efforts or who are contributing their support in ways that are meaningful to them. This marathon has taught me gratitude on a physical level. I feel it out there. It tingles up and down my spine every single morning. This marathon is about love, gratitude and celebration.

I am 2.5 months away from the starting line. So I don't have the end of the story yet. But the beginning, which started with a setback, has made this journey much more dear. And for that, I am grateful. After all, it is always about the journey.

A post-script: *Marathon day was nothing short of magical. It was perfect marathon weather, despite threats to the contrary. The first half of the marathon I ran faster than I ever have, clocking an average of 7:36 per mile—this from a normally 9-minute mile runner, is lightning fast. As I crossed the finish line, I knew I had run a PR, I knew I had beat my self-imposed 4-hour goal. And I felt the spirit of everyone who supported that journey with me along the course. My finish time, for which I am thrilled and extraordinarily grateful: 3:56:24. —Liz*

Liz was overjoyed and overcome with gratitude at the 2009 Vancouver Marathon finish line.

Your Five-to-Be-Alive for Simplifying Your Life

1. Self-Respect

You have to have self-respect to recognize, to admit that your life has become a little too busy, maybe a little out of control; that your life has been running all over you rather than you running your life. It happens. It's nothing to be ashamed of, but you have to have the confidence to overcome it, to be able to say "it's time to downsize" or "it's time to simplify" or "I am unorganized." These days many seem to be driven to do what everyone else is doing. Buy the big house, buy the fancy car, get the large-screen TV, and make sure everything "looks good." You need to overcome those superficial tendencies if they are driving your actions. It's exhausting to try to keep up with what others are doing, and it's senseless. You owe yourself more than that, you deserve better. You need to respect yourself and your family enough to do what's right and what's best for you. If you need to make cutbacks in your life to make it better or easier, then do it. Don't worry about what other people think—this is about you. It's about recognizing that you are doing too much or have too much and need to make some changes that will positively effect your mood, your interactions with family or those with whom you interact and ease the emotional burdens or stress that leading a too-busy, too-complex life can bring.

2. Happiness

When our lives are complicated, busy and we're struggling to meet all of our obligations as well as keep some semblance of order to our life it's easy to feel stressed and unhappy. Many of us get caught up in saying "yes" to everything that is requested of us. We want to help when someone asks but we have to be mindful of doing too much. When we do too much, some stuff doesn't get done. Sometimes our families get ignored. Sometimes we forget things that we shouldn't or didn't mean to forget. When these things happen it chips away at our happiness. If you can simplify your life in some way, removing from time to time or permanently a few things off of your to-do list, your happiness should increase. Stopping to think about what you can do differently in your life, what you can change or get rid of that will not only simplify your life but also make you happy is a beneficial exercise. Maybe you can hire someone to mow the lawn or clean your house—on a regular basis or just occasionally during those extra-busy times. Maybe you can plant things in your yard that will make it more maintenance-free. Maybe you can empower other family members (sounds nicer than "assign chores to" doesn't it?) to make your to-do list shorter. Maybe you can get rid of a few things that are just collecting dust. Maybe you can schedule a little "me time" so you can read a book, enjoy the outdoors or have lunch with a friend. Maybe you can order out instead of cook one night. Whatever the thing is that you can do to make life a little easier, a little less complicated and will make you feel a little happier, do it.

3. Accountability

If you identify areas in your life that need changing, that can be simplified or organized and you make a commitment to do something about it then you have to follow through. Your life will not become easier just by identifying the issues; you have to take action on them. If something seems too big or daunting or seems to require too much change, don't give up. Try to break it down and attack it in stages. Simplifying your life might be as easy, in some instances, as just saying "no" to the many requests that are made of you. Being accountable in this case is recognizing what you are actually capable of accomplishing; recognizing what your limitations are. Saying "no" will help prevent you from being overwhelmed or not being able to meet commitments. When looking at simplifying your life, being accountable means looking for a balance that allows you to get things done that need to get done in the easiest way possible. It's not enough just to identify where there are issues and where you can make positive changes, you have to actually make them happen. You have to clean out that closet, get rid of that junk, put things on the calendar so you avoid overbooking and double booking, get help from others. It can't happen without you making it happen. You don't have to do it alone but you have to be in charge of it.

4. Gratitude

Be grateful for all that you have and all that you are doing. You have to be grateful for the youth sports games that keep you running from practice to practice and game to game, seemingly nonstop. You have to be grateful for your healthy thriving lawns and gardens that take time to care for but are so lovely to be in. You have to be grateful for your home and the newspapers that get strewn about and toys that collect in the corners. You have to be grateful for the paw prints and nose prints that you have to wipe up from the floors and off the windows. There is always a root cause of something that we have or are doing and often that root cause is a very good thing. Children's schedules are often reasons why we are so busy. They are also reasons why our homes get into states of disarray. Pets can be reasons we have to clean floors and windows more often. Mother nature contributes to our ever-growing lawns and gardens. We do need to remember that even as our lives are becoming busier and in need of simplifying that all the reasons why they are this way are things to be grateful for, therefore we should feel that gratitude still as we look for better, easier ways to get things done. Simplifying is an opportunity to bring a sense of peace to our lives. We'll still be doing many of the same things we always did, but we'll be less stressed in the process. Be grateful for all that is making you feel busy and crazy and out of control but be even more grateful for the opportunity to calm it all down, to get rid of what you don't need, to organize what you keep and to bring more order and balance to your life.

5. Love

Love drives us to do things better. If our lives are too crazy, we find ourselves stressed, being short with others, tired, annoyed, upset. Those who we love deserve better than that. Think about what and who you love and then what you can do in your life to have more time to devote to those people or things. If you discover that saying "yes" to so many volunteer efforts is causing you to say "no" to your own children's activities then it's time to flip-flop those responses. If doing things you love is impossible because you are always wrapped up in some task or many chores, find a way to get help so that you can devote more time to the things you love. Love is a motivator to simplify, to become organized. If you have less stuff you have to do, then you can spend more time on the things you want to do. If you can eliminate or minimize those things that you hate to do, then you will be able to reallocate that free time to those whom you love. You also need to remember to find the time for the things that you love. It's easy to overlook the most important people in our lives because they tend to be the most forgiving of us. Don't do that. Let your love drive you to clean out, clear out, organize and schedule so that you can focus on those loves.

Other Values That Will Help You Simplify Your Life

1. Tolerance

Simplifying our lives isn't easy. There may be small changes or big changes to which we have to adapt. You must be tolerant of and understanding of the resistance you may get from others. You must be understanding of your own resistance and frustration as you make these changes knowing that in the end it make life easier and better for all.

2. Courage

It takes courage to say "no" but you have to do it to keep from getting overwhelmed. It takes courage to let go of things, to change your way of thinking and your approach to life when you downsize or simplify.

3. Generosity

Giving things away helps simplify your life. Be generous in your giving. Be generous with your time, it will take time to institute changes and gain acceptance from others affected by it. Give those other people your help and your time in the process.

4. Patience

It takes time to amass a lot of stuff. It will take time to get it all out or organize it better. You can't control everything, sometimes even with your best efforts to make life easy and organized the unexpected comes up and you have to react, you need to have patience with the process.

5. Determination

It is so easy to become overwhelmed with making changes to your life. Sometimes simplifying seems too complicated. You have to be determined to make life easier, to become more organized, to gain a better balance. The process may not be easy and it may even overwhelm you at times, but if you are determined and patient, you will make progress and you will get to the simplicity goal that you seek.

A Few Practical Steps for Simplifying Your Life

1. Minimize/Downsize.
- Material things can complicate our lives. Get rid of the stuff you don't really need, want or use.

- Bigger means more maintenance. If you are daunted by your efforts or bills for services to keep your house/yard in order, think about downsizing to something more manageable that will meet your needs.

2. Donate.
- Keep what you need, pass along what you no longer use or no longer fits.
- Regularly go through closets/cabinets/storage areas donating ill-fitting items, outdated clothes, unused gifts or items to organizations or people who can use them.

3. Use a scheduling system.
- Find a system that will help you be organized—it can be a paper-based, computer-based, a white-board calendar hung in your kitchen or office or a hand-held gadget—whatever works best for you.
- Schedule dates through this system of yours for the things that will help you simplify your life and stay organized. Put those things on the calendar to help keep you accountable and to ensure they get done and don't later overwhelm you because they've become too big.

4. Don't sweat the small stuff.
- Prioritize; take care of the must-do or important things first.
- Not everything has to be perfect. A little disarray is not the end of the world.
- Keep a clear perspective on what really matters.

5. Ask for help.
- When you have too much to do or feel overwhelmed, ask for help from those with whom you live or will support and help you.

- If financially feasible, hire someone to help you with the tasks you are struggling to keep up with.

All of the above practical steps are simply suggestions that may help you simplify your life. Everyone's life is complex in its own way. Careers, children, friends, volunteer efforts, hobbies, health issues, extended family, wants, needs, fears, etc. all play into how busy, stressed and complicated our lives can be. When looking into simplifying your life you need to remember that it is both a mental and a physical effort. There are things you may be able to change in your physical surroundings to make life simpler but you will also, most likely, need to change your way of thinking in many instances.

Helpful Tips/Resources

1. Web sites
- **www.bhg.com**
- **www.hgtv.com**
- **www.onlineorganizing.com**

2. Books/Publications
- Magazines like *Martha Stewart Living, O, Better Homes & Gardens* often include ideas and tips on organizing your home.
- Go to the library or bookstore and scan through books for ideas. Check out or buy the ones that you think will help.

3. Friends
- Ask friends how they manage their schedules or households. Copy what works for them and see if it works for you.

- Ask friends for help if you are overburdened—maybe they can watch your kids for an afternoon so you can complete a project.

4. Family
- Enlist the help of family members—get their buy-in.
- Allocate household responsibilities across the family.
- Communicate your goals and ask for assistance in sticking to them.

5. The Internet
Searching the Internet will yield many ideas, names of stores where you can buy things to help with your efforts, articles and blogs to read that relate to projects you're trying to complete or goals you are trying to reach.

Personal Story: Organizing and Streamlining My Home Life to Reduce Stress

I am Type-A. Here is some of what Wikipedia had to say about Type-A people:

> **Type A** *individuals can be described as impatient, excessively time-conscious, insecure about their status, highly competitive, hostile and aggressive, and incapable of relaxation. They are often high achieving workaholics who multi-task, drive themselves with deadlines, and are unhappy about the smallest of delays. Because of these characteristics, Type A individuals are often described as "stress junkies."*

Um, guilty as charged, at least on some of those fronts. I am impatient; excessively time-conscious, can be a workaholic, definitely multi-task, have been known to be competitive and can find myself unhappy about the smallest of delays or when the most minor things going awry. I don't, however, consider myself to be hostile (although maybe a little aggressive when I feel strongly about something), have never been one to worry about status and while driven by deadlines professionally I have not incorporated that type of process-based thinking into my personal life. I tend to have situational deadlines at home. I know sometimes, for example, that the house could use a little cleaning but it might take someone coming over for coffee to make me move that task up on the priority list. And I can relax—I love relaxing, actually, but I don't get to do it as much as I'd like. Part of that is due to being Type-A and not being able to let something else go undone so that I can relax. That's part of why vacations have become important—it is one time I'll truly relax. So, I'd say that I'm mostly Type-A and as a result I can indeed be a "stress junkie". This, however, is not a good state to be in at home. Your home is your refuge, it should be a place that is warm, inviting, comfortable—not stressful. I'd say it's still a work in progress but I've made great strides in organizing and streamlining things here at home to make for a less stressful environment.

Here were some things that were causing me stress:

- *Keeping up with everyone's schedules and being able to quickly manage or resolve conflicts/overlapping commitments.*
- *Meals – I found myself overwhelmed with making good, healthy meals most nights for dinner. It would be time to cook and I'd have no plan.*
- *House upkeep.*

- o Cleaning the house. Our house is not a mansion but it is sizeable. With three finished levels it's not an insignificant undertaking and I never felt like the entire house was clean at one time.
- o Yard care. In the warm months it's another weekly (or more) chore to keep our yard neat and healthy. We were falling behind and making mistakes.
- Organization in general. Closets were overflowing with clothes and shoes the kids had outgrown. "Stuff" was accumulating in cabinets, closets and under sinks that was no longer needed. The house that we said would be more than big enough all of a sudden was feeling too full. We had become hoarders of things we no longer needed, wanted or could use.

One thing many people do is hire out everything that can be hired out: lawn care, housekeeping, personal shoppers, food delivery, dog walkers, you name it. This is not our style, plus we are not in the income bracket to hire all those people even if it were our style. That being the case we needed to make some changes so that I wouldn't feel so scattered. Type-A people do not like feeling scattered.

The very first thing I had to do was recognize why things needed to change. I was stressed and when I'm stressed it projects onto the rest of my family. It's difficult to be happy when one is stressed. I also was feeling zero gratitude whatsoever as well. Instead of feeling grateful that my kids were active and able to participate in so many things and that we were able to provide these opportunities I was feeling put out—like everything was a chore versus a positive experience. Grateful for a nice, not-too-small house and nice sized yard? Nope, I was annoyed with the time it took to take care of it all. When it came to being responsible we were getting a middling grade—our kids nor we were missing any commitments but we were often in a rush or scrambling last minute to make sure we could honor them all. I was not being very responsible at all on the meal thing going straight to the take out menus when I had failed to plan well enough in advance to put a decent meal on the table. That was costly. I couldn't believe, when I looked back, how much we were spending on ordering out or going out to eat. It was the easy thing to do but not the best thing. So, it was time for some changes.

I made many practical changes:

- *To help keep myself less stressed about our schedules I got myself a white board calendar system that I post on the refrigerator so that I can see the most current two months at a glance. I made sure I was keeping my 12-month calendar up-to-date so I could keep tabs on all the games, lessons, appointments, birthday celebrations and vacations that were scheduled more than two months out. This "old fashioned" system works best for me whereas I know Blackberries and technical gadgets work for others. I had to find what worked for me and this calendar thing that I see every time I open the fridge was it.*

- *To help me keep up with my goal of eating out less and having more meals as a family at home I had to change my shopping frequency. I had to go weekly whether a lot or a little food was needed. I also needed to realize that grilled cheese and soup filled tummies as well as some major culinary effort that required many more ingredients. My attitude had to change on eating out—it needed to be because we wanted to go out, to treat ourselves, rather than it being the solution to my not being well-prepared or creative.*

- *To keep up with the house—the cleaning and the yard care—I also had to change my approach. Rather than wait until things had to be done I had to be more proactive and take a preventative approach. So, instead of waiting to clean after seeing that my daughter had written her name in the dust settled on the television screen (yes, to my horror, this has happened at least once), I needed to remind myself to make little efforts. Carve the house up into tasks—maybe take a floor at a time or just do all the bedrooms one day then maybe just the bathrooms the next so that everything would be clean but not seem so overwhelming or time-consuming. I also needed to realize that asking for help is okay. My husband and children are able-bodied individuals who can and should contribute to keeping the spaces they use most frequently clean. Also, paying a little for help was okay too. On the yard care we accepted that sometimes we were just too busy and we needed to call a neighborhood kid to mow the lawn. And we did hire a service to take care of the preventive lawn maintenance—things like weed control, fertilizing, mulching. We deemed this a good use of our money and it has made my husband, in particular, less stressed—thus it was doubly good.*

- *In order to better organize our household I needed to be able to let go. Literally. I had to stop telling myself that those clothes hanging in the closet from high school would come in handy for the 80's party I was surely going to be invited to one day and that every little scribble my children made didn't need to be saved and ditto on the formula-stained baby clothes. I come from a long line of hoarders—we keep everything—be it for sentimental reasons or because "we or someone we know might use it one day". My thinking had to change. Aside from the two times a year I did go through a cleansing ritual—right after Christmas and right after school started in the Fall—I needed to make a more regular effort to clear things out. It is now a monthly thing. Even if it's just one bag of stuff to take to charity, I make myself go through closets and drawers and put things aside that are ill-fitting, worn out or haven't been used/worn in a very long time. There are still times when I come up with nothing but I make myself go through the process anyway. It has helped get rid of the clutter. Things don't fall out of closets or cabinets when I open them. I can find things I'm looking for more easily.*

But why are these things even important? Well, they were important to me because they were affecting my mood, my temperament, my overall happiness. My personality is such that I needed to improve the state of my household on these fronts or I'd be tense all the time, which is unhealthy. It makes me happy to have an organized home and to sit down with my family for a dinner that I made for us all. And when things are messy or unclean, I feel irresponsible. For some being accountable is hiring people to take care of things you cannot get to, which *is fine, but that was not the total solution for me. I had to recognize the state of disarray in my life, how it was causing me to be stressed and unhappy at times and then take the steps needed to change that. The practical steps are only one piece. Aside from following those I had to look to my values to keep me on track, to make me take those steps. Every day I have to ask myself "what needs to be done" and make sure my values are where they need to be in order to address those needs. Prioritizing is important. Also recognizing that it's not the end of the world if the dust waits another day is important. I can't let the thing I'm trying to overcome get me down as I work towards making it better. I don't always have that meal planned. I don't always have a neat and tidy house. I don't always have the unused stuff in the car ready for charity when it starts to overflow. But I've made progress, and it has made a difference. Our home is our refuge. It is our safe haven and it should be comfortable and as stress free as possible. When I am **happy**, feeling **accountable** in my household role, caring for those that I **love**, and am in a **grateful** state for all that we have and all that we are afforded the opportunity to do, I feel good about myself, my **self-respect** soars. Stress is minimal and the good times roll. It is a never-ending process but I've found that if I keep moving forward, or at least not moving backwards, in my efforts then I am meeting my goal of minimizing stress.*

—Amy

Your Five-to-Be-Alive for Weight Loss

1. Self-Respect

If you don't respect yourself or *care* about yourself, about your health, about what you see in the mirror everyday then you will not succeed with your goal. Right now it doesn't matter so much what got you to the point of wanting or needing to lose weight, what matters is that you want to do something about it *now*. The first step is knowing that you are worth it. And the great thing is, once you start seeing results, when you start losing that weight your self-esteem will start to increase. You will notice physical changes, some tasks may become easier. You may breathe easier going up those stairs. Your pants will button more easily. You will feel better about what you see in the mirror. All of these little victories will help you boost and maintain respect for yourself, which will help keep you going until you reach your final goal.

2. Happiness

Most likely if you are seeking to lose weight there is some aspect about yourself with which you are unhappy. It might be that you don't like the way you look; the way your clothes now fit or don't fit; the extra physical toll it is taking on your body; the fact that you are risking more serious health issues. If you want that number on the scale to register a little or a lot lower, then there is room for improvement on your happiness meter. It's important not to dwell on what is making you unhappy, but to focus on what will make you happier. The answer is not "I will be happier if I lose weight." That's too simple. You need to understand what it is you will be happier with and stay focused on that, on those motivators. Your motivator might be that you want to turn your husband's head when you walk into a room like you used to; or that you want to set a positive example for your children; or that you want to be able to run a marathon or compete in a triathlon. Why is it about losing weight that will make you happy?

3. Accountability

Taking care of your physical health is your responsibility. There are many things that contribute to our expanding waistlines—some more difficult to overcome than others, such as age, birthing a child or many children, illness and injury. Those are things that can work pretty hard against our goal to keep our weight in the healthy range. They aren't insurmountable but you have to be accountable and responsible. You can't play the victim. Plenty of women give birth to children and lose the weight they gained. Plenty of 40+ year-old women stay at a healthy weight even though their slowing metabolism is working against them. Being ill or injured for long periods can be the toughest because of the physical limitations, but it's important when you have the green light to get back to the gym that you go; that you don't give into the difficulty of it. These are some of the toughest roadblocks. Others, in theory, are easier.

You have to be responsible with your diet. No one is forcing food upon you; you are completely in control of what you put into your body. No excuses. It may take a little extra time to read labels, to know how many calories and trans-fats and unnatural substances foods contain, but it is your responsibility to know what you are eating and how that impacts your weight loss goals. As the saying goes, "you are what you eat." If you take being accountable to yourself seriously then you will find it that much easier to meet your goal. You will be able to stick to your diet more easily and you will be able to admit when you've faltered. You have to be able to recognize and admit your setbacks, otherwise what will prevent them from recurring? There is no blame game. No playing the victim. Again, it doesn't so much matter why you are whatever weight you are—what matters is you are now taking ownership of your weight issue. If you approach this goal by taking charge and being responsible in your actions—by following through on your plan, you will lose weight.

4. Gratitude

Being thankful for having to lose weight is a bit of a stretch but that's not the kind of gratitude you need to find within yourself. You do need to be grateful for the opportunity to lose weight, that there are options. You do not have to resign yourself to a life of not liking what you see in the mirror or how your clothes fit or don't fit or how you can't walk the 200 yards to the bus stop without becoming severely winded. You have to find the gratitude, the opportunities to be thankful. Be thankful for the frozen meals that you've found to be pretty tasty. Be thankful for the comfortable athletic shoes that you wear when you exercise. Be thankful for kind, understanding personal trainers who may be helping you reach your goal. Be thankful for the tips you get from books, the Internet, friends that will help you stick to your diet. Being thankful for the things or people or food that will help you lose weight is as important as being thankful for every bit of progress that you make, no matter how small. If you allow yourself to lose that perspective or don't get started knowing you must find and feel this gratitude, then it will be very easy to slip into feeling like you cannot reach your goal, that it's too hard or not worth it. If you want it, it's worth it and it helps immensely to be grateful for every opportunity that helps you get what you want.

5. Love

Love can help see you through just about anything. If you love yourself enough to want to improve yourself you will become healthier and lose weight. If you love your family and friends enough—your spouse, children, parents, siblings, friends, relatives, pets—that love will help you keep going. People who love you want you to be happy; they want you to be healthy; they want you to be around for as long as you can be. Love can be a major motivator for reaching your weight loss goal. And it doesn't have to just be a love of people. Loving a sport that you've left behind because it is too difficult or tiring to play anymore can motivate you to lose weight. Loving a certain clothes designer whose clothing you can no longer wear well might provide some motivation. Think of all the people and things that you love and how those relationships, those things might improve if you lose weight. In the end, though, you have to mostly love yourself enough in order to reach your goal of losing weight. You have to know— no, believe—that you are worth every bit of pain, angst and challenge that you are going to put yourself though to get to that goal. If you don't love yourself enough, if you don't believe you are worth it then you might as well not even start.

Other Values That Will Help You Reach Your Weight Loss Goal

1. Patience

You can't lose the weight overnight. This is a long-term goal that will have peaks and valleys so you will have to practice patience through your journey.

2. Perseverance

When you hit a plateau you cannot give up. You have to keep on with your program and see it through until you reach your final goal.

3. Determination

Willpower is required to keep you on that diet or on that exercise plan. You have to resolve to fight off temptations to cheat or skip the workout. You cannot give in to your weaknesses—and you'll have them—you have to be unwavering in your commitment.

4. Courage

It takes courage to take on any plan that may seem intimidating or even impossible. Just admitting that you have let your weight get the best of you takes guts. Conjure up the nerve throughout the process to face your weight issue and to continue on your path, never letting the thought of "failing" come into your mind. Courage is always required when you do not know what a fight will entail and what the outcome will ultimately be.

5. Forgiveness

To begin with, you have to forgive yourself for becoming someone you don't want to be. However you got to being overweight is less important than forgiving yourself for getting there. Forgiveness will also come in if/when you get off track. Forgive yourself if you eat more calories than is part of your plan or indulge in a rich dessert on a special occasion. Forgive yourself if you skip the gym one day or go easy on the workout. There may be setbacks but you must forgive yourself for those and not berate or beat yourself up. Forgive and move on. If you do not forgive yourself, if you blame yourself or view your setback as bigger than it really is you will get off track and lose momentum. Don't dwell on your missteps, forgive yourself for being human and get back on your path to losing weight.

A Few Practical Steps for Losing Weight*

1. Eat healthy.
- Eat foods that are low in calories but high in the nutrients you need.
- Eat several small meals a day to stave off hunger.
- Consult a doctor or nutritionist to help plan a diverse, healthy menu that won't easily bore you. Or join a program where meals are provided.

2. Exercise.
- Get moving. Walk on a treadmill, at the mall, through your neighborhood.
- Join a gym or take an exercise class.
- Buy an exercise video or tune into an exercise channel and work out in your home.

3. Track your exercise progress on a calendar.
- Cross off the days that you work out to get a big, general picture of how regularly you are doing something.
- Notate the types of exercise you are doing on a given day. Highlight the ones you like best.
- At the end of a month tally up what you did—how many days and what types of exercises. Every month strive to meet or exceed the previous month's tally.

4. Keep a healthy perspective.
- Minimize your weigh-ins. Don't weigh yourself daily. Weekly or bi-weekly is enough.
- Remember that while your end goal is to lose weight, the journey has many benefits that should be recognized and even celebrated.
- Don't daydream about looking like models on magazine covers, keep a real world view of what your body can and will be.

5. Keep a food journal.
- Track what you eat daily.
- Highlight the foods you really enjoy and/or best fight your hunger.

All of the above practical steps are simply suggestions

that may help you reach your goal. Some may help "keep you honest," like the food journal or exercise calendar, but at the same time they can be reminders of what you like or what worked best so that you can be sure to have those as recurring meals or exercises. When you like something or it's working then it makes sense to keep doing it. Losing weight is as much about your mental state as it is about what you are doing physically. You can find a world of tips and tricks and information that can absolutely be helpful but everything you really or mostly need to reach that goal is inside of you. That's the best and most practical tip there is.

Helpful Resources

Below are a few resources that we have found to be and that could be useful to your goal of losing weight. These are just suggestions, not endorsements or recommendations, for those who like to have a wide-array of support options.

1. Web sites
- www.health.com
- www.cookinglight.com
- www.jennycraig.com
- www.weightwatchers.com
- www.oprah.com

2. Books
There is a wealth of books available on the topic of weight loss. If having a book or approaching your weight loss goal in a specific way is something you are interested in then you should research the books available and see if one may match your personality or approach to losing weight. Many books provide practical

information, diet tips, recipes and more. Books can be a helpful resource and support mechanism for many.

3. Friends
- Enlist friends who have weight loss goals to join you in your efforts.
- Enlist friends to support your efforts—ask them to help encourage you, to take walks with you, to ask how you're doing with your goal.

4. Family
- Communicate your goals to your family. Ask them to help keep you on track. Ask them to have a positive attitude relative to your weight loss efforts.
- Make exercising together as a family a priority or goal if possible.

5. The Internet
- Tracking your progress on a social networking site might help you remain accountable—Twitter or Facebook are two options.
- Find an online support group—being able to communicate with others who are seeking and working towards the same goal as you can be uplifting.
- Keep an online journal or blog tracking your progress.

Before you begin any weight loss program you should consult with your doctor.

Personal Story: Losing That Baby Weight

*I have two children for whom I am very **grateful**. Everything you go through to have a child is absolutely worth it. Not everything, however, related to the process is necessarily wonderful or desirable or for which I hold nostalgic feelings. The weight gain, for example, was something I could have lived without. Completely worth it, but who wouldn't opt to be right back to their pre-pregnancy weight immediately after giving birth if that were some sort of check box we could mark in the whole process? We've all seen those women—the ones who carry their babies seemingly all in their tummies and who, a week or two after giving birth, are back in their yoga pants looking ready for their magazine photo shoot. Most of us are not those women. I most certainly was not.*

Having been thin my whole life it was a bit of a shock accepting how quickly and how much weight I was gaining with my first pregnancy. Even though it seemed to be genetic—my mother and sister both gained a lot of weight and had babies weighing in the upper 8-pound range or larger—it was still a shocker. My sister and I both weighed 10 pounds when we were born and my sister's son was almost 12 pounds! So, it appeared I was headed down the same path. My son was actually born 3 weeks early and yet he weighed 7 pounds 9 ounces and I had gained a total of 55 pounds in the process. Two weeks after his birth I was still 35 pounds over my pre-pregnancy weight. I had never been in a position to have to diet before so it was an odd feeling and I felt a little overwhelmed by it. 35 pounds was a lot of weight. I had to lose more than four times the weight of my son. It seemed daunting. My plan? Diet and exercise.

Admittedly, I had an easy birth so I was feeling pretty good within days of coming home. Good enough to walk on the treadmill; good enough for some very low impact aerobics. I followed the doctor's orders in terms of how much activity and what kind of activity I could do but I wasn't about to use my just having had a baby as an excuse to put off the inevitable. I wanted to get out of my maternity clothes and back into my old clothes. It was important to me to feel good about myself and to start taking steps as soon as I could to get there. To make a long story short, within three months I was back to my pre-pregnancy weight*. I was asked by women and men how I did it. What did I eat? How many calories a day? How many fat grams? How much exercise? What type of exercise? When did I exercise? I couldn't give specific answers to some of these questions. Yes, I made a concerted effort to eat healthy and limit my intake of calories and fat. And I did exercise almost every day. The answer to how I did it, however, was more about who I was versus what I ate or what exercise I did. Even more so after my second child was born and I gained a whopping 65 pounds! At that time I was five years older, not in as good of shape as I had been, my metabolism had slowed a bit and I now had more responsibilities to juggle so more stress and less time for the physical activity. I did lose all of that weight too and in the same manner as the first time but again, the keys to my success had nothing to do with anything you could see.

When you gain that much weight you look like a very different person. True, I had a "good reason" for the weight gain but when that good reason was now sleeping in a crib and not in my tummy I saw things a whole lot differently when I looked in the mirror. I was happy with my body before I was pregnant and with all those pounds *to lose afterwards I was not. As an exhausted mother it would have been very easy to make excuses—being too tired and not having enough time to exercise would be hard to dispute as I was both. But that was not the **accountable** route. That was the victim route. I didn't want to be making excuses I wanted to be getting healthier and back into my clothes again. I **respected myself** too much to not make every effort I could to get to where I wanted to be. I was ready and willing to accept the possibility that I couldn't get back to that place. I was older; my body had changed with two pregnancies. But what I wasn't willing to accept was a bigger me without giving it my all. I knew I'd be **happy** with myself, with what I saw in the mirror if I reached that goal. I was so very **grateful** to have had the great fortune to have these two children. I told myself then that I had to be grateful for the opportunity to be in the best shape I could be for them. Kind of a stretch but sometimes we have to recognize the not-so-obvious when it comes to gratitude—to be grateful for whatever opportunities you have. You're here, so be grateful even if what you're spending a lot of time focusing on in a given moment is eating healthy and exercising. And who are we living for besides ourselves? For those we **love**. I felt to be the best mom to my kids I had to be able to get up and down with them on the floor without difficulty; to chase them around the room or be chased by them when we played; to set a good example of a healthy lifestyle; to minimize the risk of disease, such as diabetes that runs in my family. I want to be here for as long as I can with the ones I love so that was a motivator. These values were driving forces in my success. They are what kept me on my diet when I wanted to cheat; what took me down to the basement almost every night (and sometimes also in the morning) to walk, run, hit the stepper or workout* *with an exercise DVD. Ultimately I lost the weight and got into good shape—so I met my physical goal. I certainly learned a lot about the power of one's values to really push you on, how they make you stronger, how they keep you going even when you don't want to go on.*

I didn't do any crazy diet or any new-fangled exercise regimen or pay for a pricey gym membership. Not that these paths are ill-advised, it just wasn't my approach. I cut back, read labels and was careful about what I was eating. And everything I did exercise-wise required no equipment. I did use equipment—the treadmill for running/walking (a road or sidewalk would have sufficed), a step-machine (bleachers at a school or the stairs in your house also work) and a workout DVD (you just need a floor for all the exercises it contained). So in truth, I needed nothing but myself and my values in order to reach my goal. That is something I think people are sometimes missing—the "what" that is inside of them that is really the secret to their success.

*results not typical- but possible

—Amy

And before we wrap up we wanted to share just a few more of our personal stories that we think many of our readers will relate to.

Personal Story: Coming to Terms with Being "Just Mom"

I enter into any conversation about being a working mom versus a stay-at-home mom with great reluctance. For one thing, many stay-at-home moms would jump all over my first sentence saying it implied that stay-at-home moms don't "do work". Moms are very sensitive people when it comes to these kinds of things. I've been on both sides of the mom equation. I've worked full-time, high stress, high-paying jobs, and I've been the full time stay-at-home mom. Both are impossibly hard at times and both are incredibly fulfilling. There have been times when I wanted neither job and wished I could jet away for a month to a deserted island with a few good books and a butler to bring me unlimited margaritas for the asking. Some stay-at-home moms spend too much time worrying about the fact that some think they lead "The Life of Riley" and some working moms spend too much time worrying about people thinking they are doing some disservice to their kids by holding down a job. Here's the truth of the matter: all of us moms are doing the best we can do, in whatever ways we have to do it, to give our children the best upbringing we can. Sometimes being the best mom we can be means recognizing what we, as individuals, need too.

I will readily admit that it was difficult to give up my career. Living in the Washington, D.C. metropolitan area there are lots of professionals around and seemingly everyone I met would ask, "So, what do you do?" or

"Where do you work?" There was this assumption that I must have a job. I am not sure if it was because of the high cost of living that a dual-income family is assumed or because where I live is such a professionally rich area but the questions did make me a little uncomfortable. I did feel like when I said "I don't work. I stay home with our kids." that what I was saying was "I'm just a mom" or that I was somehow diminishing the value of that role—as if it was something to be ashamed of. I don't know why I felt that way. Sometimes it was the reaction—a very uncomfortable "oh" or a pause in the conversation that lasted just a shade too long as if the person just realized we don't speak the same language and therefore couldn't communicate. There were the almost patronizing responses of "oh how lucky—that's the best job in the world" said with a tone of "don't feel badly…" I didn't however, fall into the trap of feeling like I somehow had to make being a mom sound professional or phrase my role as a mom as something that was on par with being the Chief Financial Officer of some major corporation. I had heard women do this and they sounded almost bitter or overly competitive or lacking confidence. I had to admit, though, that sometimes I have felt "less" simply because I knew I was capable of having a career and being a mom but was opting not to. Working women didn't make me feel that way, I made myself feel that way and I knew I needed to snap out of it.

*First of all I had plenty of **self-confidence** and **self-respect** to know that a job did not define who I was. It didn't make me more interesting, smarter, funnier, nicer or more of the "anythings" that really matter in life. I needed to remember that.*

*Second of all, I **loved** my children—they were the whole* *reason I quit my job. I didn't need anything more to tell me that what I was doing was right.*

*Third, instead of feeling strange or less interesting or inadequate as a result of not having a high-powered career I decided to focus on being **grateful**. I was grateful to have the good fortune to make this choice; to be able to stay at home with my children. So many people do not have that option; working is a need for the added income. It is true that I was grateful all along but I was not focusing on that and I had to shift my focus.*

Fourth, it made me happy to be at home with the kids. Some days more than others, mind you, but happy nonetheless. I was happier at home with them than I was working and having someone else care for them. They, too, were happier with that arrangement.

Shifting work gears to be home with their children brought Amy's values into clarity.

*Lastly, I felt it was the responsible thing to do. Had I felt it was more responsible for me to continue working then I would have. I felt, however, that I needed to be **accountable** to myself and my family and in this case that meant doing what my husband and I felt was the best thing for our family. Working parents are not irresponsible but in our situation* *responsibility meant looking at our situation, the choices we had and opting for the one that would best meet our needs and our wants as a family.*

Sometimes "coming to terms" with something is just about being comfortable with who you are and not letting the outside "noise" get to you. The "mom wars" will always exist. I've been on both sides and one is not "better" than the other, both are exceedingly difficult at times as well as incredibly rewarding. Moms (and dads too) are pulled in many directions and you have to be able to understand what you are capable of and, more importantly, what you want to do and be. It was a much easier decision when I decided to let my values help guide me in that decision-making process.

—Amy

Personal Story: My Mentor, the Marathon

I'm a marathoner. I've trained for four, completed two, and am training now (as I am writing this) for my third finish line in May 2009. They have all been journeys that had no guaranteed outcome. I trained for two that I wasn't able to run. The first of the two attempts was interrupted maybe a month before the marathon by my needing surgery on my toe for melanoma. And the second marathon attempt was brought to a screeching halt three weeks before the starting line by a stress fracture in another toe. It was heartbreaking to miss out on that one in particular. I was in my taper period. All the hard training was finished. But if I ran the marathon, I risked causing myself to need surgery midway through the course.

The first 26.2 miles I completed was New York City, one of my favorite cities, in 2005, and just participating and finishing was an indescribable and overwhelming experience. I was slightly injured in this race so I didn't set any land speed records. I had hoped to run my first marathon in four and a half hours, but by mile three my IT band pain started kicking in. I was determined to stay steady and finish. Running through all five boroughs kept me distracted, and the throngs of New Yorkers cheering us all on, kept me buoyed. By mile 22 when I stopped to get liquid, my IT band was so irritated it was difficult to start running again. So I just kept going until the finish. Which was on a slight uphill! But a glorious experience overall. Despite my turtle-esque 4:45 finish, I was a marathoner!

My second marathon in 2007 was incredibly joyful on a different level. I was much stronger in training and didn't come into the marathon injured. This one was in Vancouver, BC, my other favorite city. The crowds are much smaller in Vancouver than in NY, but the chill in the air and the stunning coastline scenery kept my inspired and my pace brisk. I was thrilled to run this one in 4:03.

I am currently training for Vancouver again this May. I have high hopes that this one will be an amazing, wonderful experience as well. I ran my first two marathons as charity fundraisers for an aunt and a friend to raise money in their honor for cancer research and support for ALS patients. This marathon is incredibly personal. I am running this also as a fundraiser for an aunt, for ovarian cancer. We promised each other on my last visit with her before she died that we would run this one together. She loved Vancouver, too.

Each marathon has been a journey of hundreds of miles training, mostly solo, and countless hours deepening my understanding of myself—what is important to me, where my sources of strength are, and experiencing those a-ha moments that are just as juicy and powerful as the endorphins.

Want to know what one of the biggest tools in my training bag has been? Values. Yep, right along with extra sleep, rigorously good nutrition, potent yoga, periodic sports massage, proper footwear, good podcasts and running tunage, are values. The same five key values that guided me through the other challenges in my life got me to the finish line. And in ever faster times.

Self-respect plays in to my training because I want to keep improving. For me, running is my sport of choice, and I aim to be a healthy, consistent runner for decades to come. Despite my aversion to numbers in other areas of my life, I do have goals for my finish times. My fastest marathon was 4:03:47, which I was thrilled about, and my goal this year, at 40 years of age, is to run a sub-4-hour marathon. It may or may not happen, but I do want to be the best runner I can be, and I train with finish time goals in mind. We all want to be better animals, don't we?

Accountability is nakedly present in marathon training. If I put in the miles and the training, it shows. If I don't, it shows. And when I don't make my miles for the week, I feel bummed and disappointed. Sometimes I just needed more of a rest, or my schedule didn't allow for as much training as I planned, but it's all a balance. If one week is light, I add a bit more to the next week. Marathon training does require a bit of a life change. I get up at 5 or earlier every morning to get my runs in before work. I get tired early and as the miles increase, I need more sleep. My body uses sleep to repair itself. And it needs the proper balance of nutrition. I am rigorous about preparing and consuming the most nutritious balance I know of runner fuel foods I need during the months of training. These marathons are meaningful for me. Preparation takes a good third of a year. I'm excited about my time goal, and I am happy to invest the effort to get there.

Happiness is such a direct values guide. Running makes me happy. I feel physically good; it is my mind-time, my meditation, my inspiration time, and it is my best stress-relief. I'm happiest in the running groove, when my daily and weekly patterns are tuned to my training rhythm. I'd also venture to say the people in my life also are happier with a happier me. Sometimes my Cinderella bedtimes seem vexingly early, but hey, farmers sleep and rise with the sun and what better way to greet the day than in tune *with mother nature's rhythms?*

Gratitude *is something I practice with every step. Particularly because I've been sidelined with injuries, I am acutely grateful for having the health and strength to run. I don't take that capability for granted. Running and reaching the finish line are huge accomplishments in themselves, but I find the entire experience exponentially more meaningful because I dedicate each marathon as a charity fundraiser for someone dear to me who lost their health. As I mentioned above, the first was for the American Cancer Society in honor of my mother's sister. The second was to an ALS chapter in honor of a dear friend of my family. And this one is to the Ovarian Cancer Research Fund in honor of my father's sister. I am grateful to be able to run for those who can't.*

*And then we come to **love**. The final of the five values training tools. I love me, so I do what I need to do to keep my body and soul in a healthy balance. I love the people dear to me, and I run to keep me in the best mental, emotional and physical shape I can be in so that I can bring the best of me to those relationships. Also, I love running.*

The miles I log are necessary to make it the finish line. But the values I train with are just as necessary to make that journey.—Liz

Personal Story: The Values of a New Start

In my early 20s for several years I was in what everyone around me thought was a most unwise relationship with a boyfriend who dreamed big but didn't back them up with any significant time, energy or financial investments. He also didn't have the best track record with fidelity. Yet, I persisted at being in our relationship because I was attracted to him on some level. But I think in looking back on it, I was more in our relationship to learn a lot about myself and what I was made of in a condensed period of time.

The extremely edited history of our relationship is that I attempted to support us financially by working retail and by racking up close to $40,000 in debt while he was to be responsible for growing our video production business. Our business never truly existed, never got off the ground, and after months of toxic co-existence, I was confronted with the evidence I needed to walk out and let his newly-discovered (to me) other girlfriend pick up the pieces.

Except the pieces that needed picking up were mine. I thought I was at the lowest point in my mostly charmed life the night I confronted him with evidence of the other woman. The next morning, a couple who were friends of mine from work, came over, helped me pack my things, and took me in to live in their spare bedroom until I got financially on my feet enough to rent my own place. I'm still convinced they are literally angels.

I was heartbroken, betrayed; my trust in men was shot; despite having such amazingly compassionate friends, I sometimes felt unbearably alone; I wasn't sure how to get financially back on track; I had no apparent opportunities to get out of retail and into my profession of choice; I had a temporary home (thankfully) but needed to find one of my own eventually; I was ashamed, embarrassed and felt like I was tarnished goods.

When I was little, my mom didn't want me watching much TV. But two of my favorite shows were Captain Kangaroo and Sesame Street. I'm not sure which one this was on, but I kept remembering this film clip that I adored as a child of these swans or ducks all milling about on the ground. And one of them starts running and flapping his wings while these song lyrics accompanied his efforts: "…you've got to pick yourself up, dust yourself of, start all over again. …" And what do you know? That determined bird gets airborne! I still remember the tune, the refrain and the image of that duck to this day. That's precisely what I had to do after this breakup.

What I started to discover in my process of picking myself up, dusting myself off and starting all over again were the 5-to-be-alive values. I didn't know them as such then, but they were ever-present in getting me through the mess and on to a life better than I dared imagine then.

Let's break it down:

Accountability*: I had been responsible for keeping us afloat, but now I had to be accountable for a whopper of a debt that wasn't just mine. Nevertheless, it was in my name and since he wasn't going to make any payments and my legal options were limited, I had to pay it off. I had to accept my role in the relationship in allowing myself to end up in that wretched situation. Blaming him was only going to perpetuate my living in resentment and anger… it wasn't going to allow me to move forward and start anew. So, there were concrete ways I needed to accept accountability, and there were emotional levels on which I needed to be accountable. It didn't happen overnight, but once I owned my responsibilities, I could move on. AND, very important, not be in that kind of relationship ever* *again.*

Gratitude*: It took time for gratitude to evolve as well, but I was abundantly grateful to be out of that toxic life. Even though everything before me was unknown, and sometimes lonely and scary, it was a far better place to be than in the prison I had been in. And I cannot adequately articulate how grateful I was to my friends for providing me a surrogate home during my transition.*

Self-Respect: *This was and is a key player. I knew my friends and family had serious misgivings about my relationship with this guy but they also recognized I had to live my life and make my mistakes. I was aware of how foolish I had been, how much it had cost me (and those who cared about me), and what precious time I had lost to this situation. I was ashamed, embarrassed, and felt stupid. Not constructive. What truly rose from the ashes of this relationship was my self-respect. I found my self-worth, I found my backbone, I discovered how strong I was and how much I could blossom in a positive environment. I will never allow anyone, particularly me, to put me back in an unhealthy situation like that again.*

Happiness*: Once I started putting my pieces back together, and once I began to see that there was a whole new world out there for me to be a part of, I grew lighter and happier with each passing week. And instead of feeling like I was wearing a boat anchor all the time, I started to feel like me again. I started to be the me that laughed and saw things as possible and exciting again instead of seeing the world as out of reach, desperately out of reach. Literally, I started to come back to life. And I was ecstatic. Life is too precious not to celebrate joy when we feel it.*

*And perhaps the most challenging value for me to come to embrace was **Love**. I had no problem loving friends and family. But me? And potentially other boyfriends? Not so fast. With a liberal amount of time and some awkwardness along the way, I forgave myself and started to love me again. I was, I thought, pretty nifty. And once I crossed that threshold, I was ready to stick my toe in the love pool again. I had several short-term forays, but I've found one I love more than I knew I could.*

It was a journey of coming back to life. Literally. I had lost Liz in the muck and struggle of those years in the toxic relationship. But I found me, and I sprouted beyond my wildest dreams, thanks to these potent Five-to-Be-Alive values. —Liz

Personal Story: Overcoming the Adversity of a Significant Health Issue

I was twelve years old the first time I passed out. It was the first day of school of my 6th grade year; my first day of middle school. It would be the first of hundreds of times that I would faint for the next twenty-five years. It was not until I was twenty years old as a student at The University of Virginia did they discover the reason for my fainting and even then they would not be able to prevent it.

I remember that first time very clearly. It was very early in the morning on that first day of 6th grade—still dark out if I recall correctly. I was standing in front of a mirror in my sister's room while my mother curled the back of my hair for me. And then the next thing I knew I was on my sister's bed coming back from wherever I had just been. I had passed out and my mother had managed to get me to her bed. I am sure I scared her to death. I didn't know what had happened. I missed my first day of middle school.

I imagine I went to the doctor that day although I don't specifically recall that visit. There would be so many trips to doctors through the years; so many tests, needles and questions and as many negative or normal results. They all run together but the outcome was always the same: whatever they were looking for they never found. Aside from getting to know our family doctor very well, I saw my fair share of specialists. The possibilities were many for why I was having these spells. Were they seizures? Was I diabetic? Hypoglycemic? Epileptic? I was a skinny girl—bony even—due to genetics and a crazy metabolism, so was that a problem? Was I too skinny?

My blood pressure was very low which often causes people to faint but why didn't I get dizzy? Why was there no warning? Eventually it was determined, after they found nothing "wrong" (other than, you know, the fact that I lost consciousness, on average, once a week), that I would "grow out of it." I was hitting puberty, having begun my period the summer before 6th grade. We were told that a young girl's changing body can cause 'side effects' thus it was decided that must be it—my fainting was a reaction to the changes happening inside of me. Absent any other diagnosis or finding that could be the cause of these spells, it was deemed that puberty was the culprit. The resolution? I had to wait it out.

As I waited and waited and waited I had to learn to deal with a lot. This fainting thing could have defined who I was or it could have been just something I had to deal with. Like a cold. A cold that lasts twenty-five years. I was "the girl who faints" to those who didn't know me. To everyone else I was just Amy who occasionally fainted.

I am not really sure how I managed to not let this condition own me. I believe I have to credit greatly the manner in which my parents handled it and me. They never let it be something that prevented me from doing the things I wanted to do. I know that while it was an ever-present issue, it was not a constant topic of conversation. My parents did everything parents would do for an ailing child—they took notes, took me to doctors, worried, researched and probably hoped and prayed a lot. Most importantly they never let me feel like I wasn't "normal", that I should be afraid, embarrassed or self-conscious. Fainting may have been something I did but it was not who I was. I really don't remember there being any limitations put on me or on the activities in which I participated. I am sure there were but the way my parents dealt with my condition was most certainly a key reason why I did not shrink into the background and let it eat me up.

As you can imagine, having to endure this issue during middle and high school was a bit horrifying. There I was, in those formative years, having to literally be helped up off the floor as I walked to class, in the middle of class, on the track at practice or in the lobby talking to friends. It was embarrassing. I hated it. All of my friends were so great though, most of them knowing exactly what to do when I passed out having witnessed all the steps many times. I'd hear later how some even took charge well before any adult arrived sometimes telling the adults what to do. It would have been understandable for my self-esteem to have taken a hit; for me to have emotionally retreated to protect myself from the embarrassment I felt. Instead I developed a pretty thick skin. I had to.

In a high school of two thousand students it was inevitable that rumors would get started by people who didn't know me but who saw me lying unconscious in the hallway. I was pregnant, on drugs, anorexic, bulimic, faking it, epileptic, dying or had just had an abortion. And these were just the rumors I was aware of. I got used to overhearing people say things like "Is that the girl who faints?", "What's wrong with her?", "How embarrassing!" or "I would kill myself if that were me!". Having to endure those kinds of comments and untrue rumors actually made me stronger. It strengthened my character rather than weakened it. It is why I truly do not care what other people think of me. Of course I want people to see me for who I am and hope that I am viewed in a positive light but if a catty, mean, untrue, rude or otherwise unkind comment or thought arises about me, so be it. I learned who I was a long time ago and that someone else's misinformed or recklessly unsupported opinion means absolutely nothing. Words can indeed be powerful but only as powerful as you let them. I learned to rise above the noise.

The frequency of my fainting spells was at its peak from 7th-9th grade. We were trying all sorts of things to try to head off these spells. Nothing worked and everything was a nuisance but I came to accept it as that, a bother and nothing more. It was, of course, more than that but that designation worked for me. Now, don't get me wrong, there were times I got very upset. I wasn't a complete rock or a prime example of grace under pressure every time. When the embarrassment meter registered to a level that was a bit higher than normal I'd often lose it. There were times I'd cry—sob almost—in my room alone to let out the frustration, the embarrassment, the anger and disappointment. And there were times when it did prevent me from doing things. I had to withdraw from races in track meets having passed out too soon before having to run; I missed school functions and social activities. These were small disappointments but disappointments nonetheless. Then there was the realization that I was viewed as "different" by some; not a good kind of different. This resulted in another kind of disappointment for me that made a lasting impact.

One vivid memory that stands out is from my freshman year in high school when a boy I had a crush on stopped me in the hall a few days before our double date with one of my and one of his close friends and told me that he thought that maybe we should just remain friends. "Okay, sure", I said. I was confused, disappointed, hurt.

I couldn't figure it out. I thought I had done something wrong. What had changed in a week? Since I was wise enough to know that high school romances often end before they start I conjectured that he must have decided he liked someone else more than me. My friend, no longer able to bear the beating I was giving myself, told me the real reason he wanted to be "just friends". It was because of my fainting. He had apparently seen me pass out or unconscious and it scared him. He was worried I would do it on our date. "What would I do if that happened?" he had wondered aloud to his friend, adding "That would be so embarrassing for me." I am not sure I've ever instantly gotten over someone but that is what happened that day. "So embarrassing for YOU?" is what I thought. Are you kidding me? He would not be the only boy to think that way about me due to my fainting but he was the first or the first that I knew of. It gave me a little insight as to how people with real disabilities, ones more markedly noticeable and challenging than mine must feel when they are judged or treated a certain way because of something over which they have no control. I got an unexpected education when he rejected me. I became very aware of how people treated others. Tolerance takes on a whole new meaning when you've been on the receiving end of a lack of it.

What I received from being on the receiving end of intolerance or fear is a great capacity to empathize with those who live with any sort of disability or adverse condition. People do judge you in unfair ways because of their own fears, their own selfishness. I empathize with those being judged and treated unfairly and find pitiful those who act in ways that are so close-minded and lacking in intelligent thought. I think I became a better person in many ways when I was treated unkindly or with intolerance. Out of the bad was coming some good. I am not sure I realized that at the time when I was on the receiving end of the bad, but over time I recognized it.

Over the course of high school, my fainting episodes subsided. They did not stop but they decreased in number. There was no rhyme or reason to anything about them. They might come in spurts then not occur for weeks. They could happen in the morning or afternoon or night. I think we stopped trying to figure out a pattern when we saw that the data would look like a Jackson Pollack painting if we managed to connect all the data points in some logical manner. It wasn't logical what was happening to me. I went off to college with the hope that somehow a change of scenery would make a difference but with an expectation that the fainting would continue and I'd have no idea if or when it would happen.

At college fainting became a whole new experience. Why? Because the 'safety net' that I had had up until then was gone. It had become something that was known about me in middle school and followed me through high school graduation. I had almost become comfortable with it as being a part of my life. I didn't have to explain it to anyone, people knew and those that didn't could be filled in by those that did. I really didn't have to talk about it. But now I was in college, at a university with more than ten thousand students. There were probably less than twenty students at the university who would have known of me and my fainting situation and how likely was it that I would I run into those people in a sea of thousands? I was starting over.

As had become normal for me, I didn't think about my fainting anymore until it happened. I don't know when the first time was my first year but it did happen and it did freak out my roommate and other girls on my floor. The explaining began. They came to understand my situation but never really got used to it, and then my first year of college was over. Second year began and I was living in a new housing facility where I knew no one. I was starting over again. I think the first time I passed out it was on the stairs as I was leaving the building early in the year and someone called an ambulance. My second year, though, would be a turning point for it was the year in which they would discover the cause of my fainting.

At an ER visit due to a horrible stomach virus where I was very ill, dehydrated, feverish, weak and vomiting seemingly nonstop, a resident who had been looking at my chart was intrigued by all the visits to the ER as a result of my fainting episodes. He began asking me questions and I gave him the whole story. To make a long story short he recommended a visit to a cardiologist and after a test called an echocardiogram, which would allow them to see my heart functioning, they saw on the screen what my heart was doing that it wasn't supposed to be doing. They saw that I had mitral valve prolapse (MVP)—a condition where, basically, the 'flap' in my heart valve moves back and forth rather than just one way like it is supposed to. That was just the beginning. After another test it was determined that the heart condition wasn't the actual reason for the syncope, the medical term for fainting, it just contributed to it. It was not until after that test, called a tilt table test, where I was hooked up to all sorts of machines and monitors that they saw exactly what was happening to me. I actually lost consciousness in this test and they were able to see my heart valve functioning abnormally causing my blood pressure to drop to 0/0—it was so low it registered no blood pressure at all on their machine. The conclusion? That there was a momentary stoppage of blood flow due to my heart condition that resulted in a quick and severe drop in blood pressure causing me to pass out. My blood pressure was already unusually low to begin with so the drop, being so fast and significant, caused me to pass right out without the benefit of a warning, like dizziness or lightheadedness, to allow me to react in a way that might stave off the loss of consciousness. And so the hypothesis was that for all those years the MVP combined with my low blood pressure was what was ultimately causing these fainting episodes. And in the end we never did find any way to stop my fainting. Medications to treat the MVP didn't help and we were not able to get my blood pressure to rise enough via various means to stave off the spells when they came. I resolved to live with it, as I had always done. They had become so infrequent that I determined the risk of injury (or worse) from fainting was one I'd take over continuing to try medications that didn't work, made me feel strange or that might have adverse or even dangerous side effects. Now at 40 I can't recall the last time I passed out. I know it could happen again but I stopped thinking about fainting long ago—while I was still doing it quite frequently—so it's pretty easy to not think about it now.

*When I look back, it is so easy for me to see how the Five-to-Be-Alive values really saw me through or played a significant role in allowing me to persevere. I am quite grateful for much of what I learned from the whole experience. To overcome the adversity of such a condition is an accomplishment—overcoming or coming to terms with any sort of difficulty or struggle is. Something that I know helped me do so was **self-respect**. I had to have confidence in myself, to know who*

*I was to keep the embarrassment, the rumors, the not-so-nice comments or rejections by potential boyfriends from allowing me to turn inward and basically go into hiding so as to best avoid the unpleasantries of fainting. I also learned to be **accountable** in ways many people don't normally have to. I had to be mindful of what I was doing, realizing that doing some things were riskier for me than others, thus I had to choose to not do those things, even when I wanted to. My fainting caused me to miss classes, tests, appointments, meetings, or to be late for things. I had to have a brutal honesty about something I didn't like talking about in order to be accountable to myself and to my commitments; to ensure my reputation of being a responsible individual remained intact. I also recognize that the **accountability** of my doctors, my parents and others who felt compelled to support me or help me was incredibly beneficial to my well-being both physically and emotionally. They helped teach me the importance of being accountable. I was and will be eternally **grateful** for the way in which my family, friends, teachers, bosses and others supported me in so many ways and didn't make me feel different or unable to do anything I set my mind to. I am also grateful for the many doctors who never gave up trying to figure out the cause of my syncope; their perseverance and caring never waned. And I know that had I not **felt loved**, had I not **loved myself** I would have never gotten through those hundreds of episodes without wanting to just go to sleep and not wake up at night. I knew there were people that, no matter what, loved me. I may have hated this aspect of my health but I **loved so much about life** that it truly helped minimize the negatives of my condition. I too realize that I was **happy**. I have had so many reasons to be happy that the upset, unhappiness or defeat, even, that I felt at times was overcome by all that was going on that made me* *happy. I didn't stop living life. I was always aware, yes, of what the reality of my situation was but it did not stop me from having fun, from having friends, from pursuing athletics and activities that I enjoyed.*

All those years of fainting could have made me a very different person than I was then and than I am today. I am certain that my values, and in particular the Five-to-Be-Alive values, are what have allowed me to overcome all the adversity that came or could have come with that and have allowed me to thrive in this happy life I lead. Values empower us to overcome and to become more than what we can ever imagine.

—Amy

Chapter 7 — Let's Recap

One of the key messages, if not the key message, to take away from this book is that you are equipped with everything you need to accomplish anything you set your mind to. There is no fancy potion or magic ingredient that you can purchase from some shopping network or infomercial to make you whole or that will turn you into the person you want to be. Your values—specifically your Five-to-Be-Alive values—are right there inside of you waiting to help you get out of life everything you want. They are waiting to empower you to seek and achieve your best possible life. They are present—if you take the time to notice—in all of your accomplishments. You utilize them—maybe not all at once—but you do utilize all of them in the course of working towards your goals—in the planning stages and in every step along the way until you reach your desired outcome.

We don't expect you to be done with our book once you've reached the end; something that will be placed on the shelf to gather dust. Like with any book you read, some of the details, descriptions and explanations won't stick with you on the first pass. You'll remember the chapter but not all the bits and pieces and some of those bits and pieces are pretty important. Our minds are pretty amazing, holding a universe of information, but we can't be expected to retain everything. Even now, as you're just about done, there is probably something that you can't recall quite clearly or completely, so we thought we'd just recap what the book has provided. Do you really need this? I mean, you just read it for goodness sake, right? Maybe not, but we find it helpful and we wanted to offer it to you as well.

Our book is meant to be a resource, something that can be picked up and referred back to as we look to make changes, improvements or tackle old and new challenges in our lives. So if you find yourself doing that, you can turn to this chapter and quickly be able to find where you need to look to get that example you were looking for, that definition you wanted, or other ideas to help you get to what you are trying to accomplish. And if you're one of those folks who likes to read the last chapter first, well then hopefully your interest will be piqued to start at the beginning after you read this recap.

Here's an abridged summary what we now know and where we can find it again. You may want or need to flip back through these pages to reinforce or remind yourself of how our values are the essential ingredients for living our best lives:

Chapter 1—Values: The Basics—What Are Values and Where Do They Come From?

- *What Values Are.*

- *How values impact our behaviors/reactions to positive and negative situations.*

- *What or who influences what our values are and how we practice them.*

- *The definitions of 10+ important values and examples for understanding them.*

- *An understanding of the difference between values that cause real, lasting impacts on your life versus what is superficial and offers a temporary/false sense of well-being.*

Chapter 2—Benefits to Living a Values-Driven Life

- *An awareness that life is about relationships.*

- *An understanding the types of relationships we have in our lives.*

- *An education about what it means to be in relationships with ourselves, family, coworkers, friends and members of our community.*

- *What you can expect out of all these different relationships when you choose positive values practice within them or when the absence of such exists.*

- *The personal and relationship benefits of being values-driven.*

Chapter 3—The Core Five—Our Five-to-Be-Alive Values

- *An introduction to the Five-to-Be-Alive values.*

- *An understanding (with a yummy cookie visual) of our best life design.*

- *An in-depth description of what each Five-to-Be-Alive value means.*

- *An understanding of what being in "alignment" with these five values means.*

- *An understanding as to "why" these five are the key ingredients to living our best life.*

Chapter 4—Seeing Our Values
- *An understanding of what values we live by.*

- *An understanding of how in line we are with those values.*

- *The provision of a Values Map for readers to assess their values practice.*

- *A personal values assessment for each of the Five-to-Be-Alive values.*

- *An understanding, through the use of real-world examples, of how we use some of our Five-to-Be-Alive values as tools for personal benefit.*

Chapter 5—Personal Values Plans—Blueprint for Aligning with Our Five-to-Be-Alive Values
- *An understanding of how a Personal Values Plan can help you reach your goal.*

- *How to create a Personal Values Plan (PVP).*

- *A deeper understanding of the "how" through the provision of a sample PVP.*

Chapter 6—The Five in Practice—Reaching Your Goals

- *Nine different areas of our lives that we often seek to change or improve are addressed and the Five-to-Be-Alive values are applied to each area.*

- *The areas addressed are: Better Health, Green Living, Improved Financial Station, Realizing Our Dreams, Better Relationships, Career/Work Improvements, Finding/Preserving Love, Simplifying Your Life and Weight Loss.*

- *Practical steps and additional resources are provided for each topic.*

Values Gals Personal Stories

- *Our own personal stories are sprinkled throughout Chapter 6 detailing how the Five-to-Be-Alive values have helped us overcome a challenge, set us on a path to a goal or helped us reach a goal.*

- *These real-life stories provide inspiration and proof of how our approach can work for you.*

More Than Words—A Summary of Reusable Assessment Tools and Hands-on Efforts to Help You Reach Your Goals

- **Gratitude Board/Vision Board** *(Chapter 3—Gratitude section)—A creative means of truly being able to see what you are thankful for. Vision boards* *can be created to remind us visually of things we love or are happy for as well.*

- ***Daily Gratitude Journal*** *(Chapter 3—Gratitude section)—An activity that you can create online or in a bound book. Putting things in writing is a discipline that reminds us of that which adds meaning to our lives. On days when we are down we can turn back through the pages to get a lift from those daily reminders we took the time to write about.*

- ***Values Map*** *(Chapter 4)—A reusable tool that allows us to assess where we map with our values. Are we on the green end of the scale which indicates we should keep going with what we're doing or on the red end that indicates we should put a stop to our current values practices? You can use this tool again and again to assess how you are doing and whether you need to make any changes to do better.*

- ***Five-to-Be-Alive Values Assessment Surveys*** *(Chapter 4)—A reusable assessment survey that provides a set of questions allowing you to rate your values practice on a scale of 1-10. You can assess at set intervals to see how you have improved or if you have slid backwards in your positive values practice allowing you to set the goals you need to set for where you want to be.*

- ***Personal Values Plan (PVP)*** *(Chapter 5) —A step-by-step guide to help you plan for and reach any goal you want to attain. The PVP helps organize your goal, plot out your course and helps hold you accountable to the goal you want to reach.*

In many ways we view our book to be the ultimate self-help book. Why? Because we've identified and underscored what is already inside of you that can help you get anything you want out of life. We are not dictating to you what you have to get or how, exactly, you must be in order to be happy, in love or grateful. You've already got what you need. We're just helping you realize what your own gifts are and how to exploit what you already own and what belongs 100% to you—your values.

Too many self-help books, in our opinion, try to wrap everyone up in the same neat little package. That, actually, is not so helpful. Our values belong to us, and they are largely what make us, as individuals, unique. Sure, we all have values that may be similar to those of others and that are even practiced similarly, but everyone's values mix is unique. To get the most out of any self-help book you must first know thyself. That's what we're helping you do here in a big way.

It would be reckless or certainly irresponsible of us to try to claim that no matter what an individual's station in life, their gender, race, financial well-being, physical well-being, personality, social status, marital status, job, education, history of life experiences and so on don't play a role in the way values are practiced, the importance placed on one value over another, and the unique impact that can result from those practices. Fortunately, we aren't claiming that. What we are claiming is that no matter what all of those factors are, all of us are equipped with the values we need, and we are equipped with the ability to grow and strengthen those values to live the kind of lives we desire. We do not discard all that influences a person's life and thus the way in which they put their values into practice. Knowing all of that is important in understanding who each of us is; it is important in understanding how challenging getting to our end goals may be.

It is vital to remember that everyone's path to getting to a goal may be different. Some may take more steps and take longer to get there. People pursuing the same goal may have a different view of how challenging it is or may determine that it takes different values practices for each of them to get there. We know that, and we have taken that into consideration in our approach.

We are very different from each other in many ways—in our approach to writing but also in our approach to life. We share many of the same values but we value things differently so it makes sense, then, that our practice of values varies from one another as well. We do, however, completely agree on what the Five-to-Be-Alive values are and how our values and the way in which we practice them are the key to living our best lives.

Now it's time to take action. You have been given a lot of information to work with and a lot of ideas to help you make the changes you want to make in your life. We will leave you with a few more ideas on how to get started:

- Make a list of the goals you want to reach or challenges you want to tackle.
- Prioritize that list.
- Vow to get started with your number 1 priority.
- If you find you can handle more than one thing at a time, add more once you're sure.
- Using our book and whatever pieces make sense to you and for you, act!

And just a few more thoughts:
- For those of you who want to do things by the book and not leave any steps out, our book provides that approach. You can do everything we've suggested in this book and the way in which we suggested doing it. If you're type-A (like Amy) this approach might work best for you.

- For those of you who like to take what is "you" and leave the rest behind, you can do that too. If you like using surveys, have at them, if you prefer doing vision boards, create to your heart's desire and put them all over your house. If you're a more creative, type-B person (like Liz) this may be the best path for you.

Finally, we want you to succeed with your hopes and dreams, overcome challenges and reach the goals you have in life. That's why we wrote this book. We believe the key to doing all of that lies within our values. And we're not done, either, just because we're done writing this book. We will keep pressing on with our values efforts, and part of doing that is offering support to our readers. You can always reach us through our web site *www.thevaluesgals.com*. We hope to hear from you.

Happy journeys!

AMY & LIZ

Liz Stubbs (from left), Spencer Christian, and Amy Bailey after their appearance on View From the Bay.

Additional resources from the Values Gals:

Maximize Your Values: They Count in Everything You Do (iUniverse, 2001)

I am always looking for new ways to reach business associates with fresh thinking on ethics. An important subject in this post-Enron era. I liked this book for two big reasons.

First, it doesn't "preach" based around a specific religious creed. Second, it doesn't use the fictional formula that so many business books are following today. You know - somebody has a business problem that's about to wreck their career and their life, but they're saved by a mysterious stranger. Ugh!

Maximize Your Values lays it all out in a more common sense approach to the subject. I think these two ladies make an interesting point - that we all need to "talk" out loud about values. It's important, but it's often a subject that we shy away from. They offer several "Values Dialogue roundtables" as ways to get the ball rolling. And they work! I've tried using them with some friends, and it is surprising how easily it broaches the subject and gets people to open up.

If you're looking for a different approach to the subject, then this book would definitely be of interest.—R. Shaw (Amazon.com review)

For values tools and resources referenced in this book as well as blogs, daily wisdoms, workshops and the latest Values Gals press and appearances, please visit: www.thevaluesgals.com.

NOTES

NOTES

NOTES

NOTES

NOTES

NOTES

NOTES

NOTES

NOTES

NOTES

NOTES

CPSIA information can be obtained at www.ICGtesting.com
Printed in the USA
BVOW08s0830110814

362412BV00007B/32/P